WITH TEGETTHOFF AT LISSA

THE MEMOIRS OF AN AUSTRIAN NAVAL OFFICER 1861-66

Maximilian Rottauscher

Translated and edited by Stuart Sutherland

Helion & Company Ltd

Helion & Company Limited
26 Willow Road
Solihull
West Midlands
B91 1UE
England
Tel. 0121 705 3393
Fax 0121 711 4075
Email: info@helion.co.uk
Website: www.helion.co.uk

Originally published by Helion & Company 2010, in association with Iser Publications.
Hardback edition 2015

Designed and typeset by Farr out Publications, Wokingham, Berkshire
Cover designed by Farr out Publications, Wokingham, Berkshire
Printed by Lightning Source Ltd, Milton Keynes, Buckinghamshire

This English translation © Stuart Sutherland 2002
Original edition: As part of *Als Venedig österreichisch war. Erinnerungen zweier Offiziere*
edited by Paul Rohrer, published Stuttgart 1913.

ISBN 978-1-909982-65-9

British Library Cataloguing-in-Publication Data.
A catalogue record for this book is available from the British Library.

For details of other military history titles published by Helion & Company Limited
contact the above address, or visit our website: http://www.helion.co.uk.

We always welcome receiving book proposals from prospective authors.

Contents

Introduction to this edition

The imperial Austrian navy which fought and won the signal victory of Lissa on 20 July 1866, during the so-called Seven Weeks' War of 1866, has in recent years been subjected to more detailed scrutiny than has hitherto been its lot, and it is with an eye to following this trend that I present the following translation of part of the memoirs of one of its officers.

Maximilian Rottauscher, the author of this account, was born in Vienna in 1844, the son of Karl Rottauscher (born 1812), an Austrian army officer who served in the Hungarian campaigns of 1848/49 and rose to the rank of major general before retiring. Max was destined for the fledgling navy, since after the lost 1859 war with France and Piedmont it was undergoing some expansion because of fears about designs in the Adriatic Sea by the new kingdom of Italy. In 1861, therefore, he was assigned to the frigate *Novara* as a cadet. After a brief instruction, he was transferred between a number of vessels and endured a period of enforced shore leave before being assigned to the schooner *Saida*, in which he made a voyage to Greece in 1863. Further service on training ships followed, before in 1864, as a midshipman, Rottauscher was sent to the North Sea as a replacement for a casualty on the frigate *Radetzky*. The *Radetzky* was one of a force of Austrian warships present during the Second Schleswig War, during which Austria and Prussia were allied against Denmark, and Max took part in the closing campaigns of this conflict, which he describes.

But the greatest adventure of Max's life was two years later, when as a brand-new sub lieutenant and stationed on the frigate *Adria*, he was at the battle of Lissa. His description of this action, where the Austrians under Wilhelm von Tegetthoff trounced the Italians under Carlo di Persano, is extremely valuable not only because of its immediacy but also because relatively few personal accounts of Lissa have been published.

Max continued in the navy after Lissa, and his career was quite eventful. During the early 1870s he was an officer on board the corvette *Fasana*, which sailed around the world, doing considerable ethnological research in east Asia and the islands of the Pacific. He then was involved in the limited naval force established to coordinate with the army during the 1878 occupation of Bosnia-Hercegovina, and he also made another world cruise before becoming commander of an armed ship and sailing the Atlantic.

By 1894 Max had been promoted captain, and that year he was given command of the frigate *Donau* and ordered to sail to southern Africa and North America to train midshipmen, for *Donau* was primarily a training vessel. The voyage lasted over a year, but when Max returned home in October 1895 he was in trouble. At Cape Town, South Africa, he had had the ship's band give a concert, and among the selections was a march which commemorated a Hungarian revolutionary. Now the imperial authorities were very much concerned with displays of disloyalty by Austro-Hungarian subjects, and by one means or another (one automatically thinks of members of the crew with a grudge against their captain) they were told about Max's indiscretion. Emperor Franz Josef himself was outraged at the license taken, and so on Max's return he was summarily hauled before an investigation. This did not achieve anything, but he was subjected to such great criticism that he transferred to the retired list. One of his subordinates on *Donau*, who thought Max "one of the more experienced mariners in our navy, who possessed many good qualities," was outraged at his transferral and the "offensive, nay brutal style" in which it was carried out.

But nothing could be done, and Max subsided into civilian life, although it would seem there were some guilty consciences over his treatment, for he was appointed Austro-Hungarian consul in Florence, Italy, for a time. He then returned to Vienna. At some point he and his brother Ferdinand, who had been a cavalry lieutenant and had served with distinction during the 1866 conflict, decided to publish their memoirs. The reminiscences appeared in 1914 as part of the popular *Memoiren-Bibliothek* series published in Stuttgart, Germany. Entitled *Als Venedig österreichisch war. Erinnerungen zweier Offiziere*, they went through four editions until 1916. That which appears here is the section of Max's memoirs from 1861 to just after the battle of Lissa in 1866. Max also included a short history of the Austrian navy prior to 1861, but I feel it is out of place and have omitted it.

The brothers were aided in their endeavour by what we today would call a ghost writer, one Paul Rohrer, who seems to have changed the brothers' style so much that bibliographic catalogues list him as the author, and I must confess that translation was difficult because of Rohrer's convoluted style. Nonetheless, Max's account is a very interesting picture of the Austrian navy in the early and mid-1860s, its comic and harrowing scenes and its depictions of foreign lands and the adventures he had there. As usual, I have added footnotes to give modern equivalents in measurement and place names and for biographical information, vague references and the ships on which Max served. In so doing I made use of the following sources: for biographical material, *Allgemeine deutsche Biographie* (55 volumes and index, Berlin, 1875–1912); Austria, War Ministry, *Militär-Schematismus des kaiserlichen Heeres für das Jahr....* (Vienna, various years); *Deutsche Biographische Enzyklopädie*, edited by Walther Killy et al. (10 volumes, 1 supplement, indexes, Munich, 1995); *Österreichisches Biographisches Lexikon 1815–1950* (54 parts to date, Graz, 1957–); Antonio Schmidt-Brentano, *Die österreichischen Admirale* (3 volumes, Osnabrück, 1997–99); Constantin von Wurzbach [Ritter von Tannenberg], *Biographisches Lexikon des Kaiserthums Österreich* (60 volumes, Vienna, 1856–91). For ships, Karl Gogg, *Österreichs Kriegsmarine 1848–1918* (Salzburg and Stuttgart, 1967); Laurence J. Sondhaus, *The Habsburg empire and the sea: Austrian naval policy, 1797–1866* (West Lafayette, Indiana, 1989); for naval terms, August Niemann, *Militär-Handlexikon, unter Mitwirkung von Offizieren der kais. deutschen und des k.k. österr-ungarischen Armeee, insbesondere des kgl. preuss. Generalstabes und des k.k. Geniestaben, sowie auch der kais. deutschen Marine* (Stuttgart, 1877); for place names, the 1: 100 000 German general staff maps of World War 2.

Stuart Sutherland

1

As a pupil on the *Novara* and *Huszar*

It was bad to be a child 60 years ago. The household axiom was that children had to love their parents apodictically, and if they did not they were thrashed. People outside paid no attention to their delicate age and as yet delicate health. In the spring of 1861 we were taken to Triest[1] as embryonic naval officers. We were perhaps but 14 or 15, and according to the notions of the time we were treated pretty badly on principle. Our superiors decided if we would some day be worthy to wear the emperor's uniform and sword-knot by the way we developed physically. Before you rose to wear a gold lace bar on your arm, you had to live a life in which you competed with the men, even though they were already strong adults. As a result, many youths soon died or developed lung disease and were simply dismissed as unsuitable for their chosen calling.

In order that what follows be understood correctly, I have to say that we only suffered physically under conditions which in a more liberal age would have been resented. We felt it hard if we had to hunger, if we had to be torn from sleep to go on watch, but the workings of a delicate psyche were foreign to us. It goes without saying that the officers saw pupils and midshipmen as being put there to be oppressed, and so it also went without saying that we accepted our fate and dealt with it, in our childish naivety ignoring the profound importance of such maxims by mad acts, pranks and leapfrog. The whole world was like that, and the practice was named absolutism. The constitution which had just then been regranted[2] had then not a sign of putting down roots; it was like a wandering little craft in the tide of events. So as to remedy by extremely hard recruiting a lack of young sea officers, we were taken from the interior, stuffed into pupils' uniforms and divided among ships, one to the frigate *Schwarzenberg*,[3] another to the *Karolina* sail frigate,[4] a third to the *Bellona*.[5]

---

1 Now Trieste, Italy. It had been an Austrian possession since 1382 and was the empire's main commercial port.

2 On 26 February 1861, by imperial decree, a constitution was granted to the empire which established a bicameral legislature whose lower house was to be elected by provincial assemblies. The legislature assembled two months later, but fewer than half its seats were filled because of boycotts by various national groups.

3 Launched 1853, the frigate was 2 600 tonnes with 48 guns and 498 crew. She was present at Lissa and was hulked in 1869 as a training ship.

4 The *Carolina* was built in 1814 as the *Adria*, being renamed in 1821. At 914 tonnes, 20 guns and 169 crew, she was disarmed in 1864 and sold in 1870.

5 Built between 1840 and 1842, the *Bellona* sail frigate was 1 520 tonnes and mounted 42 cannon, with 332 crew. She was stricken in 1868 and broken up between 1902 and 1903.

I and three others received an order to go to the frigate *Novara*,[6] at Pola.[7] We were to learn theory and practice in a short time, for it was not seen as desirable we should be held up with much study. The fleet was almost fully outfitted and ready to bar by sea the way to Garibaldi,[8] from whose dangerous idealists and childish charlatans an insurrection in Hungary was feared.[9]

Our first impressions of our chosen profession were very bad. As the Lloyd[10] steamer carrying us entered the naval harbour in the gloomy May weather, we stood close together at the rail, frightened and with the large, uncomprehending eyes of children. A fine rain hid the town, which lay deep in the gulf, and we could see only the grotesque Roman ruins and the menacing defensive works. *Novara* had been pushed out to sea by a strong southeast wind and had had her rigging and mizzen mast (the rearmost of the three) damaged, and her deck was a confusion of tangled ropes and huge wooden blocks used to finish repairs. When the new arrivals had been rowed across, they crept on board, where reigned a seemingly frenzied, extreme confusion, hammering, shouting back and forth and the trilling of bosuns' pipes.

The midshipmen's mess in *Novara* was four metres square,[11] lit by two side lamps the size of fists, and to enter it we had to stumble down the darkest stairs in the world. The air was stifling, and a lantern burned gloomily in a corner; the senior midshipmen lay snoring on their faces on benches. When we dared to give the alarm by our steps, they began to shout well-chosen swearwords, secured their possessions, and then at once contentedly fell asleep. Only when the watch changed did this group of troglodytes begin to crash about, yawning, and then we new arrivals, by now totally intimidated and trembling, our backs pressed against the wall, had a new outbreak of rage directed against us, were scrutinized and had our sea chests rummaged. There was but one reason for this searching. "Communism" was correct and a good custom, but what happened among people of the same age was a tax on the juniors. We did get many of our things back, but by then most were useless. Good-naturedly they apologized for their condition; we saw our borrowed things with serious faces and in our egoism demanded they be mended. There was no

---

6   The *Novara* was one of the navy's more famous ships, for between 1857 and 1859 she had made the first Austrian circumnavigation of the globe, collecting a mass of scientific and ethnological material. She was built between 1843 and 1850 and was 2 500 tonnes, with 53 guns and 558 crew. Converted to a screw-propelled steam frigate during 1861 and 1862, she fought at Lissa and was hulked as a training vessel in 1881, being broken up in 1898/99.

7   Now Pula, Croatia. Although an important settlement in Roman times, Pola then sank into insignificance until 1850, when the Austrian navy made the port its principal harbour over Venice. Thereafter it rapidly increased. The harbour consisted of a northern, commercial, part and a southern, naval, part.

8   Giuseppe Garibaldi (1807–82), an Italian "professional revolutionary" who had engineered much of the unification of Italy and who was now agitating for the Italian-speaking parts of the Austrian empire to be brought under Italian rule.

9   Between the end of 1860 and the spring of 1861, the Austrian government was seriously alarmed by a host of rumours that supporters of Garibaldi would land on the coast of Dalmatia to support rebels in Hungary, which was then seething under imperial rule. There were in fact preliminary meetings between Garibaldians and Hungarian exiles, but they came to nothing, and by the latter date the scare was over. Nonetheless, as Rottauscher says, the imperial authorities were concerned enough to increase spending on the navy and expand it to head off such landings.

10   A merchant shipping company named Austrian Lloyd had been founded in Trieste in 1837 by bankers and businessmen. The Lloyd became the premier Austrian shipping firm, with extensive routes in the Mediterranean, North Atlantic and Near East.

11   12.5 sq ft.

brutality on *Novara*, as was common on other ships, since the head of the midshipmen's mess was Mensing,[12] later a vice admiral in the imperial German service, and he did not tolerate it. In the same way as the crossing of the equator today, it was usual that before someone passed Cape Matapan[13] he was not considered worthy, and therefore the older cadets hit the new boys with canes or ducked them until they lost consciousness. However, people on *Novara* contended themselves with lesser punishments. If the *Tanecchi* (greenhorns) behaved in an un-naval manner, they gave them the heads[14] and ate the rest.

Although we had been shoved into *Novara* so that we might learn something, there was practically no way of teaching us. Some officers were assigned this task, but they never concerned themselves with it, and so we had to learn as we could. In addition, other than the complex sea manoeuvres, service matters were treated by rigid regulations, more useful as formulas than as expressing the spirit of the service. Even with the guns – we had 24 smoothbore 30-pounders which carried to about 1 800 metres[15] – the main thing was that they should be highly polished, which made accurate sighting almost impossible. Moreover, the spikes with which they were pointed were on the command "Battery" crashed to the deck in unison. Little was taken into account of what happened on the following command of "Fire." For no correct officer could be brought to accept the idea that at that moment two men with curved knives were then to scrape away the plaster covering the shells' detonators; this sort of thing would always cause delays and disturb the pretty picture of drill. Only the reforms of Tegetthoff[16] banished this ghost; not, mind you, the drill, but they did introduce more quick-wittedness.

In general, the pupils were given no military or naval training. Our duties were to supervise a party when the deck was being washed; when the sails were being set we sat in the tops and shouted "*Presto, presto*"[17] without knowing what was happening, and on watch we stood beside the midshipman of the watch as his second and called the hours. We were even forbidden to note the men on leave, for this obviously demanded knowledge. But then we were granted the marvellous concession of four hours on and 12 off duty. A really sharp first lieutenant would have had his midshipmen on four hours on duty and four off day and night, which would have been pretty close to torture because you could not really sleep.

The best time for us new boys was always evening. The men scrapped around the deck, and there were Cossack dances, accompanied by handclapping and Italian serenades. While the Venetians sang their romantic gondoliers' songs, and especially the highly respected *canzone* which lyrically celebrated the memorable year of 1788, when the lagoons

---

12 Franz Mensing. I have unfortunately not been able to find details on his later career.

13 The southernmost point on the mainland of Greece; now Ákra Tainaron.

14 Of the fishes contained in the rations.

15 1.06 miles.

16 Wilhelm von Tegetthoff (1827–71), the most important Austrian sailor of the 19th century. Rottauscher has much to say about him later. Tegetthoff had been an Austrian naval officer since 1845, and he rose rapidly in rank thanks to his outstanding abilities and was a captain by 1861. During the 1864 campaign he was commander of an Austrian squadron which fought a Danish force, of which Rottauscher has much to say later. Tegetthoff was commander of the Austrian fleet which won the signal victory of Lissa over a much superior Italian force during the 1866 war, for which he is best known and on which Rottauscher also comments at length.

17 'Faster, faster' in Italian. At this period, the Austrian navy still used Italian extensively because many of its men spoke only that language. However, more Slavs and Germans were being recruited, and a German-Italian pidgin had developed in the fleet.

froze so hard that people could walk on them, and while therefore one party of singers immersed themselves ever more in the silvery shimmer of the moon, recalling the Grand Canal and other poetic objects, another party, of Dalmatians, immersed themselves in their well-known sailmaker. This man, as on most other ships, was a respected poet who set topical subjects to rhyme in the simplest manner. I can remember one of these songs, which splendidly represents their form. A seaman was caught by the provost in the men's baggage room, the *caponera*, in a tender tête-à-tête with a washerwoman. The next evening the Dalmatians sang triumphantly:

> The washerwoman came on board
> She went with me to the baggage room
> But then the provost came
> And said, "What's going on here?"

Tombolas were also set up; the prizes were small, but the enthusiasm of those taking part was great. Each number had its name; thus 55 was called the two hunchbacks, 11 lady's thighs, 33 Christ's life, and names often had coarse jokes as well, which when the numbers were called out gave spice to the game.

A non-commissioned officer was told off to fire the evening gun, which had been loaded beforehand because otherwise the operation would have taken too long. The loading was in three parts, which in turn had four sub-sections, and which had to be carried out very punctually and precisely. But the end of the day, the last post, was truly poetic. The watch stood to attention, and at their side the drummer rattled away and the ships' boys shrilled on their pipes. In the breathless night the ship sailed through the Adriatic, perhaps as in centuries gone by, for each gallery still had a gilded, ornate lantern as high as a man.

While the frigate lay in Pola repairing her damages I had only two important duties, which made me not a little proud. Once I had to deliver fresh water on board, and on the other occasion brooms – in a barren country the latter were easier to find than the former. The detachment cut down the number of bundles needed from the brushwood on the shore, and then returned. The only thing the commander had to do was to make sure the party stayed sober, for every lighthouse keeper had a supply of bad wine.

While, therefore, bound up with many new things, we found ourselves living a sorrowful life with the older midshipmen and learned how fortunate we were compared to others, work on the *Novara* came to an end. The pupils had had just time enough in Pola to learn what it took to make a good midshipman. There were various things: the secret of encouraging the men when they rowed by treating them to a *picciona* (a small measure of wine), avoiding the customs and smuggling tobacco and being nasty to the officers who had transferred from the flotillas on Lake Garda or the lagoons.[18] Everyone from high to low truly harassed these strangers, which ended with them resigning or transferring to the infantry. The last and certainly most important thing we learned was the arranging of a system of credit, how many wine bonds made a 10-kreuzer[19] note and how many notes an egg bond. Such bonds looked curious, i.e., one for three eggs written

---

18   In addition to the main fleet, the Austrian navy maintained a flotilla of small gunboats on Lake Garda, in the west of its province of Venetia, to defend against possible Italian incursions, as likewise a flotilla of small craft for the defence of the lagoons of Venice.

19   The then standard minor currency of the empire; 100 kreuzer equalled a florin.

in capitals and with "So and so imperial-royal cadet" at the bottom. In those days, paper money was used even for food, and this protection was a percentage of future salary confined to one ship. Soon after we learned something of these small dodges, which can deceive people even in the worst case, our frigate sailed for Lussin.[20]

It was my first sea voyage in a warship, and the first time I saw the whole complicated apparatus of the monstrous sails functioning easily before the wind as if the clumsy three-master was a pleasure yacht. But just as we had been reconciled to their dimensions and wanted to reduce them by force of habit, death leaped onto the deck and snatched a sailor from a yard. He lost his footing by an unlucky step, and we saw him above us falling through the blue sky like a puppet whose limbs were being jerked. But just as this frightful simile occurred to us, the body crashed to the deck, where it lay shattered to pieces. The dull thud and pool of blood on the white-scrubbed planks made a considerable impression on we novices, and in our disturbed dreams at night could not think of the sight as anything more than a pale, red-irrigated cheek.

The burial of the unlucky man in Lussin harbour filled us with the most anxious nervousness. Times were hard, and they were continually filled with disturbing news from Italy. If we had the capacity of youth for enthusiasm, so we also had childhood's instinctive enthrallment for real life, that only a youth of about 20 will discard with laughter, until with age he relapses to the first days of his life. So were we moved in this still day of early summer. As the light vanished softly from the barren hills, brushwood showed on the slopes as colourful spots, and the launch with the coffin, its flag at half-mast, moved towards the shore. Six boats, their men in full dress, followed the corpse's memorable passage in slow time, and all was secluded.

We were snatched from the feeling of depression the burial left us by the severe watches and ugly fault-finding of a new commander. If we had laughed before, we were silent now, and the men's songs became rarer. A sullen mood filled the ship, and its commander was just the man to increase it daily. By the way, he showed what kind of person he was when he was commanding another vessel and ordered, "Hammocks overboard!" to lighten it. Officers and men alike felt the order for his relief which soon followed to be a deliverance.[21] *Novara* returned to Pola after this very short cruise, and to their astonishment the novices were told that they were now trained and would be matured by more thorough study over the winter on His Majesty's brig *Huszar*,[22] in the Bay of Muggia, at Triest.

Because we had had an unbelievably lazy life on the *Novara*, the new situation affected us much harder, although it was only a prelude to the most depressing thing that can happen to a young soul, namely that two years later, after the sudden cuts to the navy, there

---

20 Losinj, Croatia.

21 This man would seem to be Commander Georg von Millosicz (1819–90), who commanded *Novara* for 17 days in July 1861. Although an 1855 official report described Millosicz as "somewhat rude and irascible to subordinates," he was nonetheless regarded as well-educated and competent. Millosicz commanded the *Schwarzenberg* at Lissa and went on to become a vice admiral before retiring in 1883.

22 The *Hussar* (not *Huszar*) schooner had been built in 1813 and had been taken over by the Austrians the following year. The *Ussaro* brig from 1829, she spent 1848–49 as the *Il Crociato* in the service of the rebellious city of Venice, becoming the *Hussar* in November of the latter year. From then she served as a training ship, of 462 tonnes, with 12 18-pounders and 100 crew. Stricken from the navy list in 1868, she was sold two years later. Her captain from June 1861 to January 1866, or during Rottauscher's time on her, was Lieutenant Johann Baptist Pelzel (1830–1914), who retired as an honorary rear admiral. Given conditions in the imperial navy of the period, nearly five years was a very long time to command a vessel.

was a systematic attempt to force us out because we had become redundant. Suffice it to say the course on the *Huszar* was opened, and, as if to mark that the superficial contrast between *Novara* and *Huszar* like an unclimbable wall, we were given sailors' clothing. Crammed 50 to a cabin barely 10 square metres[23] in size, we were now separated from the few men assigned the ship by a rope curtain. I say a few men, because suddenly the pupils were forced to do tasks over which they previously had exercised a bare supervision. An especially bora[24]-rich winter made these duties difficult because our health suffered. In the early morning, while the water froze in the small wooden containers, we huddled in total darkness, washing the deck by lantern light, cleaned the guns, cleaned the pots, pans and eating utensils with freezing knuckles, and in every sort of weather washed in icy seawater in *Baljens*, large water casks, our naked upper bodies exposed to the storm. Plus the food became more miserable day by day. No officer asked what the pupils were eating, and to complain was looked on as a sign of effeminacy. The ship's cook, who was paid to provide the food, looked to his profit and did not think of us. Many times, even in harbour, we were served salt meat, and it was often pretty putrid. And when we did not eat it at midday – as hungry as we were, we pushed it away with disgust – it appeared for breakfast the following morning in the shape of a goulash. After seeing this trick but once we speedily threw the dish overboard. Once when we were exercising on the yards it was so cold one of us was shivering so much he threatened to bring us all down, and when we got to the deck we beat him to within an inch of his life. The prevailing lack of consideration on board made us callous and hard in a jiffy. Frequently totally exhausted by our duties and watches, the latter four hours on and four off, we then had to study, tired to the bone from a sea voyage, frost and wind, and we had barely fallen into a feverish half-sleep when we were ordered on deck again. The studies were a special case. The students sat freezing on their benches on the half-deck, writing feverishly, while the teacher, clad in a greatcoat and shawl, dictated as he walked back and forth. Then our books were examined.[25]

There was no daylight in our room, and the sailors looked at us behind our rope curtain as if we were a menagerie; the hatchway leading to the deck was pitch black. It could be closed but with a piece of sailcloth, and we did not raise it because then we froze miserably, for there was no heating. And so we sat in darkness, in the foul atmosphere produced by oil lanterns and 50 bodies. We were so crammed together that only some of us could sleep in hammocks; the rest lay on the bare boards between the benches, their heads pillowed on their rolled-up clothes. Rats ran over these unfortunates, and there were lots of rats on the brig. They were just as hungry as us, to the extent that one night one of my comrades had his shoe bitten through and his toe gnawed. Today, when I think back on the small room, it seems to me to be a bad dream, especially when I recall mealtimes, for my mess of eight had only one plate. While one of us devoured his food, the others bent over him, lantern in hand, on the watch for the moment when half the food had been eaten. And I have never forgotten the delightful scene when a mother of one of the pupils,

---

23 31.3 sq ft.

24 The bora is a wind peculiar to the Adriatic which can come on in seconds, blowing down from the coast of Dalmatia. It can be especially severe in winter.

25 The instructional officer from 1861 to 1863 was Sub Lieutenant Richard Pagatschnigg (1838–95), who was likewise at Lissa and died a honorary rear admiral.

a Countess St Genois,[26] came on board with a liveried servant. Her son was not then to be found, and we looked at her in wordless astonishment. Then the servant, who seemingly took us for ships' boys because of our sailors' clothes, asked condescendingly for Count St Genois' quarters. One of us took him by the arm, dragged him below, showed him a miserable bench and said with sarcastic pathos, "Here are the apartments you seek, sir."

We never saw our 26–florin[27] pay, for the first lieutenant took charge of it. He used it to pay for our uniforms and food, giving us what remained as pocket money for runs ashore. We always had something to eat, even if it was bad, and we knew where we would sleep each night. We also had to equip ourselves with telescopes and sextants if we misplaced them. That process was always very complex. Deep in the Café Specchi[28] in Trieste, warming his hands at a coal fire and wearing a chequered shawl around his neck, sat the Jew Schloß. One pupil or another sat down beside him on the faded plush sofa and began to haggle in a hushed voice. "Schloß, what will you give me?" Schloß then pushed his hat back and thrust out his lower lip. He always pleaded his poverty, that he was sacrificing his wealth out of a sense of charity, that he had been ruined for the longest time and had no more money. Nonetheless, he finally took out his wallet and gave you 50 kreuzers or a florin, and even two florins to the most persuasive. With that your debt was noted in his account book, and when the amount the depositor had pledged had been reached he sadly brought him the forfeited sextant. Schloß had a whole heap of these instruments, selling them at a good profit to merchant marine captains. When I was a pupil, and then a midshipman, he got two from me, paying only 25 florins for both of them although they were worth over a hundred. In a word, we owned only the last of the three required items of telescope sextant and ship's book, and the latter was blank. Then, as has been noted, we lightened our service as much as we could and celebrated our few free hours in stormy fashion. Right at 6 P.M., once the evening meal was over, yelling started as if a crowd of schoolboys had been let loose. We fought, cheered, shouted, pelted each other with everything possible and began to sing amusing songs in chorus.

So winter passed. The plague of rats became so bad it was necessary to fumigate the ship. The course was finished, and so in February 1862 the *Huszar* went to the New Hospital in Triest. Hundreds and hundreds of animals were found when the ship was opened, and we were touched when we saw their mass death, for hunting them had enlivened many dark nights.

On 4 March there began the examinations, which were held at the Hydrographic Institute.[29] The commission was very strict about rigging and setting of sails, but the rest was child's play. For instance, my entire gunnery examination was a question of what was to be done if a gun came loose in a storm. The answer was, "Insert a *Schwaber* (a cut-up rope used to dry the deck) and then hammocks under the wheels of the carriage."

But sadder than the entire winter on the brig was the last hour on her. About half of us, myself included, had been appointed midshipmen, which was not a great change and was signified only by an epaulette on the left shoulder. We were therefore ready to leave

---

26 Perhaps Gabriele Eleonore Josepha Countess St Genois (born 1827); if so, the boy in question would have been her stepson, Philip Ernst Moritz (born 1843), the son of his father's first marriage. The count transferred to the army in March 1863.

27 The standard large coin of the Austrian empire, replaced in 1892. It was also called a gulden.

28 The Caffè degli Specchi was on Trieste's central square, the Piazza Grande, and it is known to have survived into the 1920s.

29 This institution was closed in 1866.

the *Huszar*, for most of us were to go to the squadron, then cruising off Dalmatia. But the reckoning by the first lieutenant of the months of pay he had administered had yet to come. Suddenly there were two shots from his cabin, and when the door was forced open the officer was found bent over on the deck. He had tried to put a bullet into his brain, but the first time he only grazed himself, and when he tried again he only succeeded in shooting out his eyes. We were hastily shipped away, and some weeks later we learned that the unfortunate man had to suffer eight more days from a burden he never should have borne. His accounting had been correct; indeed, he even had a claim, since he had silently been laying by a not insubstantial sum for the pupils. He was brought to a martyr's death for nothing, by an incorrect reckoning he could not master at the last moment. Frightened he would be missing yet more, he had tried to commit suicide without checking the figures against one another.

My new ship was the *Salamander*,[30] then the navy's only armoured vessel. On the first day there were wild battles between the old and new midshipmen, and since we were so much younger and weaker we naturally mostly lost. While I always knew how to ward off the consequences of such defeats, two others were soon practically the slaves of a certain L. In the evening he had them fight each other under lantern light, while he played the flute. One of the midshipmen tried to shoot himself, but owing to prudent supervision he was seized and locked up. The other travelled between freedom and the provost, with whom he played cards, as was usual.

Following this tribunal, I was transferred to the gunboat *Hum*,[31] which was with the squadron in Dalmatia. I was pleased, for besides the difficult conditions prevailing on *Salamander*, the ship was unpleasant to the highest degree. The midshipmen's mess had neither air nor light; the toilet pump was before the mess door, perfuming breakfast with the smell of excrement. Moreover, the *Salamander*, with its projecting heads of the armoured screws, resembled a flatiron with warts and was not built in the style of that time. In contrast, *Hum* had sails, and the head of its mess was a pleasant man, Peichl,[32] who later became head of the Lloyd shipping firm. We cruised some months along the Dalmatian coast, even reaching the miserable hole of Valona.[33]

When, after serving 18 months, which cost me too much because of the hardness of the life, I received my first leave and was allowed to travel to my parents in Vienna, I thought I would fly into the air. I gave my telescope to Schloß, and after changing some notes started out with a florin and 40 kreuzers.

---

30   One of the navy's first ironclads, the *Salamander* had been built between 1861 and 1863. At 3 027 tonnes, 34 guns and 343 crew, she in 1866 was at Lissa. The vessel was stricken from the active navy in 1883 to become a depot ship, and she was broken up in 1895/96.

31   The *Hum* was one of a class of standardized gunboats constructed in 1860/61. At 869 tonnes and 4 guns, she had 139 crew and was also at Lissa. She was stricken in 1900 as a hulk, becoming a coal lighter in 1905. Her captain between March and November 1862, during Rottauscher's time on her, was Commander Johann Nepomuk Pauer von Budahegy (1830–85). He was not, somewhat unusually, at Lissa but retired as a rear admiral.

32   Josef Peichl, who went on to win a medal as part of the Austrian squadron in the 1864 campaign.

33   Vlöne, Albania, then in Turkish territory.

2

Leave in Vienna. The miseries of the reduced navy

This was the summer of 1862. In Vienna, most of the bastions were still standing,[1] and men wearing swords and ladies in wide crinoline dresses[2] were promenading on the parade glacis beneath the chestnut trees. Among them were officers, imposing in their white tunics, and the dandies of that period with their flapping cravats. You looked over the wide glacis to the suburbs, to the Neubau and Josephstadt quarters, not then part of Vienna, and in their gardens were small green inns where quartets were playing.

The sensational event of my leave was a grand rifle competition, to which numerous people streamed from the federal states, especially those in southern Germany. There was much music, many flags, much fraternization. I gulped this down in large draughts, although for monetary reasons I could only be a spectator at the garden fence. Even the Café Daum, on the Kohlmarkt,[3] was closed to me, despite my longing to sit among high society and be seen among the crowd, idle as a cavalier. The brilliant life drew me as powerfully as did the secluded side streets along the Danube, and my legs had to be strong if they were to keep me up. Then carriages drawn by white horses came onto St Stephen's Square[4] to astonish you, and soon thereafter I strolled down to the canal, where the worst rubbish of buildings served as lodgings. There on the staircases along the lanes, Jews of all professions hung out red trousers; there were colourful parrots in cages and good fruit stalls. And all in broad daylight plunged into the mediaeval darkness of the ravines formed by the houses. But to my father, I had more serious things to do on leave than wander the streets to the astonishment of many, some of whom took my uniform for a porter's, others for that of a member of a rifle club and still others for that of an attaché of the French embassy. Father took me by the hand and taught me French as we walked back and forth across the bastion. The wind blew into my nostrils; before me there lay temptingly the green band of the Viennese Woods. I would have run there with much pleasure, but Father's sharp clearing of his throat brought me to reason.

And when he left, Mother entered the picture. She had just as considerable a demand: I had to learn how to dance. I was opposed at first, but very soon I found myself in the company of some dear suburban girls. Then I saw that as the most exotic guest I had for a while displaced the most elegant householder's son as their darling, which made me feel extremely pleasant. Suddenly admired unendingly, I was the centre of the dance

---

1   In 1857 there began the demolition of the system of old fortifications which enclosed the inner city of Vienna to allow the city to expand. As Rottauscher notes, this process took some time, until the middle of the 1860s, in fact.

2   The crinoline, a stiffened hoop beneath a woman's dress, was fashionable from about 1855/56 to 1867 or so. Crinolines could be extremely large.

3   The Café Daum was during the 1850s and 1860s the most fashionable in Vienna, but during the 1870s it went into decline and closed.

4   The square in front of St Stephen's Cathedral and a prominent landmark in Vienna.

circle, and I leaped about spiritedly. The girls showered this 15-year-old's ears with sugary gabble, curtsying very graciously, holding the skirts of their white crinoline dresses in their fingers. They saw in me something romantic, perhaps something like a pirate. But to keep them unblemished, to show them the consequences of what they in their dreamy artlessness half-consciously longed for, I limited myself to inviting the prettiest of them to a glass of beer. I spent my last kreuzer on Pilsner and passed time in innocent merriment with some missy or other. And as the summer wind blew among the trees of the gardens of the inns, she vanished into the shelter of the night and the stars. She had asked that whether it was as God willed it, from many a long day to find my right way. Or she had asked if a ship could travel in darkness or if one could sleep on a ship. But then totally different people from a missy asked me questions like that; privy councillors, for example.

But where now were the steps with crinoline dresses held gracefully, where now the bastions, where the dreamlike gardens of the inns in the suburbs, with their railings, harpists and old chestnuts, and where also my dreams of heroic naval deeds, when I saw Pola again in the autumn!

While I was absent, the navy had had a so-called reduction. In the same way from month to month, after Garibaldi's Neapolitan adventure had passed by and the possibility of an insurrection in Hungary had been as illusory, the government's interest in the Adriatic disappeared. Ever since there had been an imperial fleet, it had been subject to great neglect or feverish demands, according to the political climate. The low and high points changed according to the world situation; at one time there would be commanders aged 27, at another a midshipman would have to wait eight years before receiving his officer's sword-knot. Only four men of the liberal parliament, Giskra[5] at their head, concerned themselves with the Adriatic. A short period of flourishing was followed by a decline. We named the four the "String Quartet." But they played what they were handed without a correct idea of what was necessary and what was not. That was for two reasons: the first was that it was a principle of liberalism to threaten the military, the prop of absolutism; the second was that the empire's finances were in an evil state. The illness which had devoured Austria since the days of Franz I[6] was to get at the empire by economizing. But it would have been more reasonable than instead of letting us live or die to have broken up our frigates, brigs and schooners into small pieces and sold them as firewood. At least we could have looked for another way of life. But we were tied by our oath of loyalty and were not easily satisfied. Ship after ship was decommissioned and lay as wretched, sad things behind barricades; of the entire fleet, but one frigate, one corvette and seven gunboats were manned. Work in the arsenal halted, and the midshipmen, out of work, travelled through Pola's filthy streets.[7] If you had previously suffered materially, at least you certainly had not felt a pinch, but now one came. We no longer knew what was happening to us, and three-quarters of us were abruptly set on land, paid 40 gulden in

---

5 Karl Giskra (1820–79), a liberal member of parliament from Moravia after 1861, was one of the principal supporters of a navy for coastal defence only.

6 Franz I (1768–1835), emperor from 1804.

7 While Rottauscher may be correct to say that cost-cutting governments were responsible for the navy's reduced state, it should also be remarked that the most recent work in English on the navy of this period concludes that the tendency of its commander between 1862 and 1864, Archduke Maximilian (1832–67), the brother of the emperor, was to sacrifice "all other aspects of preparedness to free more funds for ship construction," and that in consequence the fleet sailed only rarely, standards of education dropped and the level of seamanship declined, so leading to a corresponding loss of morale.

total a month and forgotten I was hit particularly hard, for I had not paid in time an amount advanced for travel. As a result, seven gulden were deducted each month, and since I received almost no allowance from my strict father, I was ruined. If I refer to my earlier remarks that what little money we did receive was not once dispensed regularly, and that often only on the tenth or twelfth of a month, it will be understood that we went to the dogs in no time at all.

Because a room was too expensive, when the midshipmen could they slept during the day or night on board one of the decommissioned vessels, where the officers' bare cabins, like the rooms of an abandoned house, gave illegal shelter. The rest of the time we drew out in thickets along the shore, where we lay on our backs or fished, sitting on the stones. In colder weather we sheltered in the so-called midshipmen's room of the Café Gaudenz on the town square. Our refuge had been built in a decayed Venetian palace and was overlooked by the Temple of Augustus,[8] and there alone we could still get credit. The café was one storey tall, along a side street; its floor was on a lower level than the stairs leading into it. On the smoke-stained walls were old coloured woodcuts, depicting Archduke Friedrich as the victor of Saida,[9] ships in the midst of waves as high as houses and other nautical scenes. It was always dark, partly because of the dirty windows and partly because of the narrowness of the street. There we sat on black divans set against the walls, in whose rips could be seen their seaweed stuffing, played cards or billiards, smoked and yawned away the day. We lived on credit, and often it happened that for a week or more you existed on black coffee, goat's milk, bread and eggs, always haunted by the piercing fear of living above your means. Every *Kapuziner* (dark coffee with milk) you ordered was a question of your fate. Usurers, who charged five gulden per month for loaning barely one, even took the clothing from our backs, for professional honour forbad leaning on these men.

In this way the midshipmen offended the port admiralty. Our smuggling on board decommissioned ships was deemed quite unmilitary, and so one fine day – we had tasted this dubious freedom for I believe four weeks – we found ourselves on the *Adria* frigate,[10] which lay moored at the Riva. We were theoretically to be taught a course, but it did not start right away, and later there was not much of it either. We continued to live our former life, with the difference that at least now we had a fixed sleeping place. The destitution of our clothing became extreme. For a long time I went about like a limping animal because my right-hand boot was missing a sole. Another boy had no trousers to speak of, and he always had to wear a greatcoat; a third kept all his property in a chest for shells of about 40 cubic centimetres.[11] We ate from tin vessels delivered from a German inn, the Angelo Sporco; the mornings and evenings were always passed in the Café Gaudenz. Or

---

8   The Temple of Augustus and Diana, built in 19 B.C., close to the shore in the centre of Pola. It is a major tourist attraction today.

9   In November 1840 an Austrian squadron was part of an international force intervening in the Egyptian-Turkish War, and after the Egyptian-held port of Saida (today Sidon, Lebanon) was bombarded an Austrian landing party under Archduke Friedrich (1824–47), a membner of the imperial house, landed and took possession of the town.

10   The *Adria*, launched in 1856 as a screw-powered sailing frigate, was 2 198 tonnes, with 41 guns and 365 crew. She was rebuilt in 1866 and was reduced to an artillery training vessel before being hulked in 1871, and then stricken and broken up in 1888. As Rottauscher later notes, she took part at Lissa and suffered some damage.

11   16.3 cu in.

we drank tea we had made ourselves and ate confectionaries, very many. Then suddenly a new giver of credit emerged, a pastry cook. What we were given as opposed to navy bread! But we also had to eat Turkish honey and Indian fowl fritters, unspeakable delicacies. We dreaded them but had to gulp them down, because the cook saw them as a security for his payment from the midshipmen's account books. When our money ran out, he took what was owed him and gave us the lamentably small amount which was left. Then we started on credit once more, for with the few kreuzers left we could not procure breakfast and supper.

Christmas was a very splendid holiday. Our last money was scraped together and we bought a sack of sweet baked chestnuts, which were twisted on a guitar string.

But I have almost forgotten one man, who deserves honourable mention by his unbounded and most ardent friendliness for one of his sort, the master tailor Tomasi from Trieste. He clothed us in the most wretched cloth. The prescribed blue frock coats were rare: instead of them he made some in black, brown and green, which at once tore and hung like wet rags about your starved body. But for all that he clothed us; he gave credit and was always one of the first to come to Pola to call in his debts. When the date for payment was known, sailing parties of several days' duration were held. We all owed money because we simply could not count and had barely saved the right amount for the washerwoman. But to pay her reckoning was considered an affair of honour. "Little Marie," as she was known, came twice monthly to Pola by the Lloyd steamer to bring and receive washing. Twice a month – for the entire navy. There was no provision in the naval harbour for cleaning the officers' white uniforms. Little Marie was, as a Viennese, pleased with me to the point of almost coddling me; she personified her native town. And the measure of the fame of this very round old person was shown in her encounter with the admiral of a British squadron. When one of the British squadrons was lying in Triest, its officers did not pay their accounts. Marie at once had herself rowed to the flagship and energetically reprimanded the startled admiral, saying that the lowest Austrian ship's boy had more honour than the British staff put together.

I have noted that a course was to have been given on the frigate, but those who were to have taught it were happier to stay on shore. Moreover, the teachers there emphasized only rigging; on anything else they were unobligingly silent. You went to the lectures or ignored them, as you liked; if the hammocks were not taken down, you could sleep until noon. The technical lectures, read by fitters, were especially neglected, by ourselves as much as by the lecturers. We looked on machinery as if we had been cavalrymen looking at the supply branch.[12] This was the more the case because the fitters were remarkable only for their extreme ignorance. For example, one had been a non-commissioned officer in the Greek army, and now he was suddenly a marine engineer. Another, who held such a technical position as a stoker, claimed he was the only real technician because he could shovel the coal into the boiler behind him without having to look where it was going – that was the heart of the matter to him. A third once stopped in mid-lecture. Then one of the pupils rose – he was older than most and had joined the navy after completing some courses – and silently solved the problem on the board. "Confound it," shouted our professor, "you can give the lectures from now on!" "What on earth for," the midshipman answered, "usually when you're lecturing I have a card party," and sat down again.

---

12   I.e., with extreme disdain. Cavalry was always reckoned the most prestigious arm in the Austrian army, the supply branch the one of least value.

This lax devotion to study had the result that the port admiral forbad us to come ashore. But now we made it a game to deceive the guards, and when the police were ordered to arrest any midshipman they met in the city, the whole thing became a martyr-like pleasure to us. Wretchedly fed, dreadfully clothed, without satchels, telescopes or sextants: that was real gallows' humour to us. Often in the middle of the night there resounded a systematic braying like donkeys, windows were smashed and to applause a new, impregnable Café zur Burg was named. Once we were sitting there playing cards when the waiter crashed into the room: "The police are here!" In a moment we barred the door with benches and tables, and while our enemies were forcing an entry the cadets jumped out a rear window into the street and fled to the castle.[13] There we lay among the Scots pines on the glacis and sang, someone blowing a trumpet over the sleeping town: "We live a free life...." This behaviour caused the port admiral to lose patience. The *Adria* was to go to a mooring buoy and hoist the quarantine flag – we did that ourselves to three cheers.

Thus until the spring of 1863 the frigate lay before Pola like a punishment ship, and soon the jokes ended. Now we had much fun, interrupting the monotonous day with "scampering," or pinching of the most refined form. In bad weather we were certain we would be exempt from duty, for the teachers crawled above the mizzen beam or the larboard spars. If a Lloyd steamer came in, everyone would man the yards and salute, to the passengers' astonishment. But the situation was unbearable; we midshipmen were real prisoners.

And then spring turned to summer, and the sun's rays burned down on the motionless *Adria*. Boredom and heat did what orders never could have done. We suddenly became passionate sailors and asked to be allowed to make a cruise, assuring the authorities we would be pleased to go even as common sailors. Our wish was for movement, distance, foreign lands. Our request was granted – there were certainly ships enough. One was summoned, and we were ordered to man it, some sailors were given us to cook and clean the toilets, and off we were sent to Greece.

---

13 In the centre of Pola, on a wooded height.

3

On the *Saida* to Greece

The ship we 56 midshipmen manned under Commander von G. was the schooner *Saida*.[1] With her masts propped up from behind and her slim lines, she resembled one of the pirate ships then still cruising the Mediterranean. She was so small there was not even room for our chests, and so our walking-out dress, caps and linen were jammed higgedly-piggledy into small oilskin bags. Since we had neither money nor a need to set this clothing to rights before going ashore, during the voyage we entered harbours in our own country and in foreign lands as if we were crashing a masked ball. Our caps had no cockades, the coats and trousers had more holes than cloth and we seemed to have been transformed into scarecrows, but after months of hunger we had to be pleased. This voyage on the *Saida* remains to me a simple, happy carnival, surrounded by the poetry of sail and sea, loving the merriest episodes which fate was pleased to strew over us. But as the guests at a feast see a seriously cold morning after a frantic night of celebration, so the end of this cavalcade was tinged with a presentiment of world history striding along, demanding to make a man of a boy and like the fist of a giant, distinguished by every nobility of feeling and thought, a spiritual hero awaiting his hour.

Our commander had a reputation for being an especial eccentric, with an insatiable thirst for action, tortured by a robber-knight mentality, but also with the extreme of what a proper man would consider as dignified behaviour. He had been a hard drinker but shortly before had become a teetotaller, and now he wanted the entire world to convert to water. His impulsiveness made him embrace his midshipmen at one moment and the next to threaten to have them shot. In short, he went through life with passion and resorted to violence whenever and however he could. His best example of quixotic behaviour was when he was commanding the brig *Montecuccoli*[2] off Megline.[3] Despite all sorts of warnings, he always ran at full pace at the head of landing parties, without pistols or escort. One evening he was ambushed by bandits, and despite his desperate resistance and gigantic strength he was thrown down, robbed and, since he had wounded one of the bandits, tied naked to a tree and beaten. Despite being threatened with death, G. bellowed so loudly with anger that he caught the attention of a well-armed company which happened to be passing by, and the robbers were driven away. But barely had G. been freed than he ran off alone into the night to thrash at least one of the vagabonds. When the uselessness of this overheated fantasy became clear to him and he realized he could not hunt for the bandits in all the bays of the Bocche di Cattaro,[4] he went to

---

1   Launched in 1855, the *Saida* was intended as a training ship, and at 334 tonnes was armed with 6 guns and had a crew of 68. She was converted to a brig in 1872 and was wrecked off the Calabrian coast in November 1874. Her captain would seem to have been Commander Gustav Ritter von Gröller, who as Rottauscher later notes also fought at Lissa.
2   Originally an Italian vessel, the *Montecuccoli* was ceded to Austria in 1814. At 391 tonnes, 21 guns and 126 crew, she was rebuilt in 1836, and then in 1868 hulked, being stricken and sold four years later.
3   Meljine, Yugoslavia.
4   Boka Kotorska, Yugoslavia.

Megline, ran through the awakening village dressed like Adam, had himself rowed to his ship and ordered his excited men to get ready for action. The guns were manned, the drums beat, and the shots of a broadside whistled over the town to explode in the woods of the coast and smash some Scots pines.

This man greeted us as if we had been the greatest cause of suffering he had had in his life. As he set off down the row of midshipmen he shouted, "Do you know who I am? I'm Commander von G. I've been captain of the ironclad *Salamander*! Me! And now on your account I've got to command this tramp! Thank you very much!"

But as delightful sunny laughter rained on the two odd characters of the *Saida*, who raised G.'s resentment into a storm to such as a wise man would not seriously think to raise himself. One was the ship's doctor, a former member of a students' society with countless duelling scars, an eternal lover of beer. He always stumbled over his sword and wheezed every breath as if it was his last. He was to teach us geography, natural history and hygiene, but I do not recall he taught us anything other than students' and drinking songs. The second odd character was the old pilot Garafolo (Carnation). His real name was Braikovich, but everyone called him Carnation because the 70-year-old mummy always went on shore with a carnation in his buttonhole. This flower summed up his philosophy of thoughtful fatalism. If anything unpleasant happened to him, he said with conviction, "Bravo, Garafolo" and never thought about it again. He had fought in 1848, and death and suffering were for him embodied in the carnation, with which, perhaps, he had some enduring memory. Garafolo's nautical knowledge was generally as fatalistic as he was. If someone asked, "Braikovich, what's that piece of land there in the sea?" he would think for a time and then say with conviction, "That's undoubtedly an island." Or if someone enquired from which direction the wind would come next day, he would just as decisively indicate the entire horizon and say, "From there."

The cruise encouraged most of us – we were delighted with the life of the lucky outcasts once more, our shoes tied to our backs, scrubbing the decks and impregnating with tar the standing items (ropes of the tackle permanently attached to the ship and supporting the masts and topmasts) and sleeping beneath the stars with a coil of rope beneath your head. Only one of us suffered. If the anchor broke loose from its moorings, be it in fine or rainy weather, whether in a storm or if the sea was like glass, this person would rush down from the forecastle, stretch out his arms and legs and vomit copiously over the side, one of the few cases of incurable seasickness whose acquaintance I made. But we others sang and were in good spirits, for we had an abundance of food. I do not believe it out of place to here describe the fate of the members of the *Saida*'s crew. Of seven I do not know what happened to them. Of the others, one became an imperial German vice admiral (Mensing), one an imperial German rear admiral (Junge),[5] 15 reached flag officer rank, nine rose to lieutenants, two transferred to the army, two to the Lloyd merchant firm and six became naval officials. Two died shortly after embarkation, one (Proch) was killed at Lissa,[6] one became a member of the Hungarian parliament, one went raving mad, two more died in mental asylums, one as a criminal in prison and the last two were killed by Mexican guerrillas while serving as officers of Emperor Maximilian.[7]

5   Franz Junge. I have likewise not discovered details on his later life.
6   Robert Prosch. Rottauscher mentions him in his account of Lissa.
7   Maximilian, younger brother of the emperor, had in 1863 accepted an offer to become emperor of Mexico, then being contended for by the French and their local supporters and Mexican republicans.

Soon afterwards we noted the first test of G.'s headstrong behaviour. We had anchored off Gravosa[8] to embark fresh water and food, and we had abandoned ourselves to the lovely but also obvious prospect of viewing the mountains of Greece when dark clouds gathered in the southeast and the schooner smelled bad weather by her first nervous movements. A drizzle began to fall, the deck became inundated and the tops of the masts disappeared into the mist. For G., the correct thing to do was to warp from the sea into the gulf. Although the anchorage was well sheltered by the peninsula lying before it, some of us soon began to comment that they did not at all relish the greasy breakfast cocoa, which made a feast for my belly, for I greedily swallowed six portions one after the other. But then a veritable storm came out of the powerful southeast, and we could see its breakers thundering on the shore. The *Saida* creaked on her anchor chain, and Pilot Braikovich, suspecting his commander's intentions, gave increasingly plainer hints about a poor sirocco and a misty sea. As he did so he walked around the deck, manoeuvring his fingers before his countenance and speaking in a loud monologue. In such circumstances, he said, we would doubtless be better sitting behind the peninsula over a glass of black wine – this was oil to the fire of G., who called the old man a cowardly woman and an ass and wished him to the devil and bad luck to him. Up rattled the anchor; the schooner, freed from its grasp, at once gave her first jolt with that impetuousness which betrays the seaman as a good yachtsman and shot through the channel, and to the sound of "Bravo, Garafolo" we slowed as we advanced into the first really bad weather we experienced.

And there the sea laid hold of us. While there came from the southeast a slow swell, overlaid by banks of clouds, their shredded edges hanging like gauzy flowers, the *Saida* bowed in passing the outlet and the next moment gave a sudden leap as she climbed a wave. The impact of the bow as she crashed into the trough sent a shiver through the ship, and spray leaped over the side and drenched my seasick comrades. Now a wave hit the side of the schooner and heeled her over as if she had been wounded, the water gushed from the spray chutes (openings for letting out water), and coils of ropes and all not used to this movement began to slide. But G. and the *Saida* were in their element. The slender vessel dug ever more greedily into the waves, climbing ever higher and crashing down faster, so that it often seemed as if the ship meant to bore through the boiling volumes, which next second opened before us as an overpowering storm shot over the deck. For the longest time, most of us, pale as sheets, hung from the things they were clinging to or were cruelly flung around like marionettes, while cannonballs thudded from their racks and played skittles with the sick boys. But in a pitiless voice G. commanded: "Take in the second and third reef of the topsail and mizzen!" But only the 10 sailors assigned us and two of the older midshipmen went aloft, all of them capable of climbing the masts as they bent at an angle of 30 degrees and carrying out this pendulum-like work without putting their lives in danger. G. cursed and raged at the sufferers, answering Garafolo's compassionate and silent entreaties with pithy names, and with a ghastly oath the commandant declared that all were to be on their legs before he turned around. Then we healthy ones fell on the sick, and since then I have thought that a thrashing is the best way to cure seasickness.

Unfortunately for Maximilian, French support was withdrawn in 1866, and in 1867 he was captured and shot by the republicans. A "legion" of Austrian troops was recruited to help Maximilian govern his new country.

8   Gruž, Croatia.

Soon afterwards there rang out the order to fall off to leeward, and with the storm at her back the schooner flew back to Gravosa.

If such a manoeuvre had the advantage of teaching something, G's next feat lacked this excuse all the more. The summer storm had passed ahead of us, and the *Saida* sailed south in an increasingly bad, seething sea. Many times there blared the alarm trumpet; grappling irons were raised; we ran to the guns, grabbed pistols and pikes and fastened dead man's knots. For the goelette was now in that area made unsafe by piratical *galanticcios* (small vessels), and we had to be on the watch, ready for anything.

Greeks on the sea, Montenegrins and Turks on the land – that was then the state of affairs in the southern Adriatic. Today piracy has died out, so that it is rare when bullets whistle around a blockhouse along the Hercegovinan frontier. Only during a hard winter, when privation sweeps through the Black Mountain,[9] do bandits ambush peasants and steal sheep. But at that time you had to be on your guard, and as late as 1869 the garrison of Fort Stanjevic, near Cattaro,[10] was massacred. Unrest had broken out in every quarter, and bands of Montenegrins came over the border.[11] They stopped a woman whose job it was to bring milk to the fort every morning, and a boy disguised himself in her clothing. In the half darkness, the gate guard was deceived by the ruse, and when he opened the gate he was cut down. The men who rushed in killed the watch and shot the men as they leaped from their beds, also killing the lieutenant in command as he rushed into the courtyard from his ground-floor room, revolver in hand. The sergeant major, his wife and some gunners were the sole ones to succeed in fleeing to the battery, and from there they fired their guns and rifles down on the attackers as long as they had ammunition. Eventually a shell fell on the flagstones of the courtyard, exploded and tore some of the invaders to pieces, on which the others abandoned the courtyard. But there was no aid to hand for the defenders, and the enemy lay outside among the rocks and waited for the time when a lack of food would force the garrison to surrender. Then the milk woman, who was from the region herself, began to negotiate with the attackers. She performed a splendidly heroic deed, and for centuries people will sing of Gusla the Victorious. Only through great courage could she cap her fine work and have the invaders allow the defenders to withdraw freely, and then not for nothing was she called a brave warrior and noble falcon.

The wild children of nature were pleased by her actions, and the only point in the negotiations which caused difficulty concerned the corpse of the senior lieutenant; the gunners wanted to take away their dead officer, but the enemy held out. Obviously they wanted to follow their customs and stick uniform buttons in the eye sockets of the corpse, whose eyes had been cut out, and then nail the mutilated body to the gate. But in the end they abandoned this act of triumph and accompanied the troops as they marched away, chatting in a friendly manner and smoking, as far as Cattaro. (I cannot of course vouch for every word of this anecdote because it came to me second-hand, but what are true are the ambush, capture of the fort and sparing of the survivors.) The most frightful circumstance of all is that many times hunger alone is the incentive for such attacks. There were bloody ambushes of provision columns in the interior on its account, and the most dangerous time for a blockhouse's garrison was always just after its meat and bread had

---

9   I.e., Montenegro, since the word means Black Mountain in Italian.
10 Kotor, Yugoslavia.
11 Rottauscher does not mention that the real reason for the unrest was that in 1869 compulsory military service was introduced in Dalmatia, and that the population rose in revolt to resist its introduction.

been delivered. One New Year's Night in the 1880s the Montenegrins left six dead in the snow in front of a blockhouse in the Lim region, on no more grounds than that the day before the gifts for the company posted there had been delivered. Despite the garrison's rapid fire, they pressed right up to the walls around the blockhouse, and the Transylvanian Romanians had to drive them back with rifle butts and bayonets.

If conditions at sea had not been as pronounced for a long time, still like things occurred. For example, on our voyage we encountered in Zante Harbour a sailboat which had narrowly escaped two Greek corsairs. But we were not fated to be blessed with a private, as G. so ardently wished.

On the other hand, there was the British three-decker *Marlborough*.[12] This colossus was steaming through the Corfu Channel, the schooner looking like a barque in comparison, as she passed by armed with 131 guns and with an admiral's flag of the three kingdoms waving over all. But although the *Saida*, in accordance with custom and manners, saluted the *Marlborough*, it was not returned, and G. was dumbfounded. We awaited the British reply, but there was none, although a good and ever-increasing distance separated us from the impolite ship. And while the schooner reversed course with a graceful turn and sped after the gigantic vessel, its commandant was already thinking of enforcing the salute by force of arms if necessary. An impudent midshipman said the other ship would lay herself close by us, have heavy tackle (blocks and tackles for raising and lowering heavy weights) laid down and raise our boat for their men's amusement. No sooner did G. hear this piece of blasphemy than he summoned the guard and wanted to shoot the frightened youth. But the midshipman was delivered as a salute broke from the *Marlborough*'s gunports, and G., pacified for the moment by the flattering crashing of cannon, resumed course and with a seigneurial wave of his hand allowed the condemned man to live.

The same day we ran into the harbour of Corfu.[13] You have to understand the state of the Ionian Islands at that period in order to understand the decline in their prosperity under the Greek regime. At that time, while it was still British,[14] Corfu was considered one of the most renowned winter stations in the Mediterranean, a sort of Monte Carlo. It had palatial hotels, was crowded with the best society, and in the capital was a 2,000-man garrison, which bestowed its abundant pay on the island's inhabitants. But the pain of not being united with Hellas was greater than the pleasure of economic well-being. I recollect our bum-boat man, Papadopulos, who gave the same reply to every remonstrance of this sort: "Today I eat beefsteaks, and tomorrow I'll eat olives." Yet at the same time he gave bad tobacco and counterfeit change for good money. It is certainly odd that we laughed at his speeches and never once though about our own Italian provinces. But Papadopulos's most bitter charge against the British was that they were swindlers. The facts of the case were: the British navy was paid every three months, and so every third month there was a chance for the Corfiotes to lay in huge amounts of all sorts of supplies. But one day the

---

12 Launched in 1855 and converted to steam power and screw propulsion while on the stocks, the *Marlborough* was 6,065 tons and the flagship of the British Mediterranean Fleet at the time (commander in 1863 Rear Admiral Stuart). Unfortunately, rapid advances in naval technology soon rendered her obsolete, and she paid off in 1864 to become a receiving ship, foundering in 1924 while on her way to the breakers.

13 Kérkira, Greece.

14 Great Britain had acquired the Ionian Islands, off the west coast of Greece, by the Treaty of Vienna in 1815, which ended the Napoleonic Wars, and ran them as a protectorate until 1864, when they were united with a now independent Greece. The islands provided a splendid strategic base.

commanding admiral became sick of the eternal demonstrations,[15] and so on the first day of the third month he sailed off to Malta with the entire squadron, leaving the Corfiotes with unpaid bills and the food and drink they had bought on speculation.

It can well be imagined that we swam over to the island with our balled-up uniforms and spent time there as far as our minimal reserves of cash would allow. We walked to the saluting gun and crowded together in the square to the music of a royal British regiment, which played splendid polkas and waltzes, for most of its members were Czechs. Our ship too was much inspected by the curious, and above all by officers, who were astonished by our 30-pounders fifth class and gave them that respect due antiques. But the crowning event was a visit by an exalted personage, the grand admiral of the Sultan of Zanzibar. One fine morning there came on board a very elegant, laughing black man with a card of introduction from the British governor. G. hid his contempt behind a mask of friendliness and had brought all that was good and expensive. His Excellency let slip that he was there to place orders for the sultan's navy, and so it happened that when this black man left the *Saida* tipsy he was saluted with 15 guns. The salute was the key to unlimited credit in Corfu for the grand admiral, which he needed very much, for he was no grand admiral and had falsified the card of introduction.

We had not yet gotten over G.'s Zanzibar adventure when a merrier escapade of cheerful tricks was played out when His Majesty's brig *Pylades*[16] ran into Corfu on her way home from Piraeus. She had been lying in Attic waters with the multinational demonstration squadron under Tegetthoff, had reprovisioned and had now turned for home with a cargo of five female circus riders. Their history was as follows. Despite the disturbed times – King Otto had just then been chased out of Greece[17] – a travelling Austrian circus had been guest stars in Athens. It had aroused very much enthusiasm in the descendants of the victors of Marathon,[18] especially as far as its lady members were concerned, so much so that one evening about 50 soldiers in full accoutrements had crashed the performance, thrashed the clowns and borne off the women with hue and cry. Tegetthoff had threatened the provisional government and had exacted such a large amount of money in damages that the circus made its best profit by that. Now the released prisoners, newly rich, were travelling to their homeland on His Majesty's brig *Pylades*.

The *Saida* left Corfu after five days. We cruised the length of Cephalonia and Zante,[19] ever more southward to our goal, the Peleponnese. Most of us still had a certain schoolboy enthusiasm for classical antiquity, which not even the lectures of one of the ship's officers had dampened. It was then that we were prepared by lessons from mythology and had impressed on us the most splendid importance of Zeus's amorous adventures. In the evening, as we sat bare-footed on the guns, smoking and squatting, we let our souls fly

---

15 For *Enosis*, union with Greece. The political situation in the Ionian Islands had been unstable for some time as a result.

16 Launched in 1849 and rebuilt in 1860/61 as a transport, the *Pylades* was hulked in 1868 and stricken and broken up in 1872. She displaced 485 tonnes and had a crew of 110.

17 King Otto (Otho) I (1815–67), a Bavarian prince, had been chosen as king of an independent Greece in 1832. However, when he attempted to discard the constitution he was overthrown by a military revolt in October 1862. The political situation in Greece then became quite unstable, until a year later Prince William of Denmark arrived to become the new king.

18 The battle of Marathon, fought in 490 B.C., was a renowned victory for the Athenians over their Persian enemies.

19 Now Kefallinía and Zákinthos.

ahead on the wind. In mid-June the *Saida* entered her first mainland harbour, Kolokythia.[20] Behind the high mountains lay Athens and Sparta, but this illusion was the only one which remained, for we were greeted by the wretchedness of the present day. A half-wild mob wrapped in ragged clothes crawled out of decaying huts to beg, from far and wide nothing to be seen but stones, boulders and sand, and a Greek gunboat lying before the town to behead robbers. It is still a mystery to me what there was to steal in Kolokythia, but let it rest at that. The excesses of brigandage had become so great that this vessel went from harbour to harbour with a guillotine settling matters on a day-to-day basis, a pardoned criminal as its executioner. From this period many a tale was recounted, and if they were perhaps not true they were believed because of the prevailing conditions in Greece. At one such execution, the condemned man succeeded in overpowering the executioner, and with the escort looking on with interest he beheaded him in his turn. He was so skilful and measured withal that there was nothing for it but to appoint him executioner.

Disillusioned and annoyed, we quickly bought the food and drink to be had in Kolokythia, and which was quickly exhausted: resinated wine, pots of honey, mutton fat, meal, flour and fresh water. More sadly and more speedily than we had hoped, the schooner left the classical coast, but not without G.'s having found a reason for another heroic deed. As the *Saida*, her flag flying, set sail during the hot afternoon, the execution ship slumbered to port, its crew below at their siesta and only a greasy white mongrel barking at us from the deck. G. looked closely at the gunboat, which made no effort to show her flag to us as we left, and ordered dryly, "Load the guns." Only one was not loaded, because it would be the visiting card for a battle. We passed close by the unsuspecting Greek; oblivious to its fate, the dog barked on the sun-washed deck. When then the unloaded gun was fired, its blast blew the dog into the sea, and soon a tumultuous mob of men looking like seamen were struggling to raise their flag. G. watched their efforts, nodded in satisfaction and considered his honour had been vindicated.

But this incident did not make him happy enough – he longed for more, and so he undertook to fight his and our pampered characters. While we were on course for Zante, a powerful north wind fell on the slender *Saida*. We had stowed the things we had bought in Kolokythia in a cabin which served as our pantry, but we had forgotten to close the porthole. When then the cook went for some food, he was astounded to encounter a pulpy mass, for the sea had forced its way in and had fused honey, meal, sugar and everything else, the mutton fat swimming on top as befitted its special characteristic. Moreover, the day before the barrel of salt meat had been found to be rotten and had been thrown overboard, and so the crew's food consisted of the following: meat – none; mutton fat – 30 pounds; cocoa and coffee – enough; sugar – none; rice and macaroni – two sacks; some cream cheese, and biscuit for six days. But although G. too was affected by this disaster, he broke into scornful laughter when we asked him to run into a port – now the moment had come to show we were men; he was sailing for Zante, and he would become a vegetarian or starve before he would put into port before then. So everyone on the ship got rice at lunch and macaroni at dinner, and our initially cheerful mood died away as we stubbornly continued on course, everyone in a decline. The day before we reached Zante we had nothing more than a soup of water and the remaining biscuit, which had been taken from a corner of the pantry and was half covered in dust and filth. In this dire need, Garafolo killed and roasted his pet hedgehog and presented him as a delicacy

---

20 Not identified; perhaps Katákolo, Greece.

to the commandant with all the pomp he could muster. The commandant fell greedily on the splendid meat. "What is this?" he asked. "That," said Garafolo sorrowfully, "is my hedgehog." Barely had the dreadful word "hedgehog" left his mouth when G. threw the plate at his head. Staggering and leaping back in superstitious fright, G. thundered that the unfortunate animal was to be at once thrown overboard. The pilot gulped, "Bravo, Garafolo," took the hedgehog by a leg and tossed it into the sea. And yet there was so much hunger.[21]

Perhaps the commandant reduced our emergency stock of provisions so much that a dangerous state of affairs did develop. At that time, many naval officers, and G. most of all, swore to the truth of seamen's superstitions, as did every sailor from the *Capostivo* to the *Gabbier* down to the lowest *Quartiglier* (these ranks in the Austrian navy had been taken from Venetian dialect and meant: *Capostivo* = cabin sailor, the assistant to a bosun who had quarters below his; *Gabbier* = top sailor, an important rank in the rigging crew; *Quartiglier* meant deck sweeper). Although they were not familiar with the Flying Dutchman or hobgoblins, on every voyage they always followed rules which could not be broken at any price. A dead man had to be given to the sea as soon as possible, for otherwise his soul would pull the ship aground like a dead weight; the killing of a cat brought a hex; to set sail on a Friday would bring strong opposition, which the officers could overcome only by disciplinary measures. St Elmo's fire was drunken sailors dancing along the yards, and as in the time of the Roman triremes, pieces of copper were sacrificed to the ghosts by being first nailed to the yard and then ceremoniously thrown into the sea to ensure good winds.

It was high time we reached Zante, and our joy at seeing the charming island was increased because we saw ourselves as survivors. If the wind fell we really starved, and every sip of wine, every bite, we considered a gift from God. We were extremely happy just to be in Zante. But in the meantime, G. brought us a new surprise, this time a most pleasant one. With delight on his face, he told us that he had received an order to join the squadron at Piraeus[22] and that six of us would be selected for transfer to the *Novara*, which Tegetthoff commanded. The names of the lucky ones remained a secret, but this news had the effect of starting a sort of epidemic of eagerness. There was only one question on people's lips, and every alternative was considered, because to serve with Tegetthoff was deemed a high honour. He had had a legendary career, and as the most junior captain he had commanded the vessels in Greece for a long time. The great respect in which he was held was based not only on the firmness with which he acted on behalf of Austria's interests in the Greek disorders with his weak force (a frigate and two gunboats), it was also because his name already had a good reputation in other navies and that his opinion was greatly valued by many senior officers in the international councils in Piraeus. Tegetthoff's hydrographic research in the Black Sea, his travels in east Africa, his adventure with the Somalis, his clash with a British admiral in Syria, and last the circumstance that his restless nature made no knowledge foreign to him – all this united with his sincere, imperturbable, tough character to form an example of the ideal leader. He knew whom he commanded, and by mixing experience and knowledge in equal amounts, he was able to demand blind obedience to his orders. As we sailed around the Peleponnese, every hour

---

21 The explanation for this incident is that it was (and perhaps still is) widely believed that hedgehogs are a delicacy of gypsies, whom many in central Europe hold to be unclean.

22 Pireás, Greece, the main port of Athens.

there came the question of who would be selected to serve on the commodore's flagship, replacing in our hearts our vanished Greek Utopia, the most fertile past remembrance. Twenty miles[23] from the longed-for harbour, the schooner encountered a stiff blow and, deeply reefed and with little prospect of being able to arrive soon at our destination, the *Saida* lay facing the crags of Attica.

Towards evening on 3 July we saw a large vessel, almost all her sails set, coming towards us from Hydra.[24] Rising and falling in the rolling seas without moving from our place, we wondered at the splendid manoeuvres of the gigantic ship. G., summing up his friendly nature in a phrase, said it could only be a mad Briton who was wasting the strength of his men in battle by behaving in such a manner. But then the lookout shouted that he recognized the *Novara*, and we and the commandant were seized with enthusiasm. While we let out reef after reef, the frigate came on like a cloud of white linen, plunging her bow into the foam of the azure sea. Hanging in the shrouds, we shouted our cheers to the commodore as he passed us as if we wanted to hurl our souls to him. But the *Novara* hoisted the signal, "Set all sail and follow!"

And so all night we clambered around the rigging, always hearing, "Let fall – reef," and then again, "Unreef." With burning eyes we looked at the gigantic phantom ship before us, which under the steely blue night sky of the south rolled convulsively as it fought off the wind and the ever-rising sea. The pipes blew and wave after wave washed over the plunging schooner, but the commander flew before us.

The *Saida* anchored beside the *Diana*,[25] the dawn guardship, in the roads of Phaleron,[26] in the middle of eight British ships. There was a real forest of masts in Piraeus Harbour, which was literally crammed with the fleets of other countries. Among them was the battleship *Re Galantuomo*[27] of the Italian navy, although since we did not then recognize that kingdom we had to call it the Sardinian navy. Chaos reigned on shore, and Athens had been devastated by pillage and street fighting. The army had considered the government installed after King Otto's flight just as guilty of murders and disease and liable for damages as had foreign nations. Greek infantry had tried to plunder the bank, and the National Guard had stopped them only after a battle, traces of which could still be seen in the flecks of blood and bullet holes. General uncertainty reigned; the short distance between Athens and Phaleron could only be traversed if you were in armed bands, and the same was true of the capital's remoter streets. Nothing was more certain than that all the money in circulation had been forged and that every tenth house was a beerhall, the first act of civilization which Bavaria had let happen under King Otto.

The day we arrived, the six selected were transshipped, and we others were given hope we would receive shore leave. We were fairly bitter, for in the past G. had never let his midshipmen go ashore. So then we sat and cleaned tables, benches and corridors with sand in order to pass inspection by Tegetthoff. Suddenly, as we were busily engaged in this task, we heard the bugler's signal from the deck above. We scarcely believed that the

---

23 Assuming Rottauscher is using nautical miles, the distance would be 37 km or 23 miles.
24 Ídhra.
25 A corvette launched in 1834 as the *Veloce*, she took her later name in 1849. At 718 tonnes, 20 guns and 188 crew, she served until hulked in 1869.
26 Paleo Falíro, Greece.
27 *Re Galantuomo* was a Neapolitan battleship which became part of the new Italian navy in 1861. She displaced 3 369 tonnes and had 64 guns, but she was not present with the Italian fleet at Lissa because of her unhandiness. She was stricken in 1875.

commodore would arrive at such an early hour and that he would come to our sorry cabin, but come he did, cap in hand and followed by his adjutants. I will not speak about his visit, since because I served under him during the most brilliant period of his command I am perhaps biased, but I will say that while we were standing at attention I at once felt an extraordinary man was inspecting us, as if he could read our deepest secrets. I do, however, know two things, which are the respect for us we could read in those warm blue eyes and that Tegetthoff was the first person who addressed us as well-bred young men since we had entered the navy. Midshipmen who had had to clean guns and wash decks shed tears of thankfulness and love – we would have protected him from enemy fire with our bodies. The hour that Tegetthoff held us under his spell and admitted us into his navy matured us a year, and it was as if we had been serving somewhere completely different beforehand.

And what a necessary complement to this meeting was the shore leave. We were assembled in a coffee house, still speaking about our commodore, drinking a beaker of masticha,[28] when a swarm of sailors from the *Re Galantuomo* pushed their way in. They had scarcely seen us when a whisper of "Austrians" ran through their ranks. One of them tried to run at us, and his comrades dragged him back – we clapped our hands to our sabres. The man howled, bit his lower arm and shouted the most frightful curses, and if the situation had not been so serious he would have been no bad comedian. The other Italians dragged the madman away, looking darkly at us, and we felt that this experience and the man, who had taken hold of our souls, were one.

But still time crawled along at its languid pace. We returned to our monotonous Dalmatian cruising, and once more the midshipmen, who were now much too old in their rank, were preoccupied with the exhausting duties of plain sailors of the time. One of them was a certain Urbancich.[29] He had been sentenced to wash the deck and addressed severely, and, provoked, he said to a comrade in a lowered voice, "If they shout like that at us we'll go slower." When the commander of the guard demanded to know what he had whispered, the frightened man repeated his words. He was brought before a military court and dismissed – midshipmen were cheap in the years of the reduced navy. Urbancich roamed about unemployed for a while, and then entered Emperor Max's service and so became one of the two hanged by the Mexican guerrillas.

Another midshipman and I were assigned to the *Arethusa*,[30] then Pola's harbour guardship. The winter was very harsh, and from time to time a dreadful bora would make the Triest lighthouse a mass of ice up to 20 metres.[31] We kept warm by means of cannon balls, which we heated red-hot in the kitchen and placed in containers of sand. And then I was once more transferred with the majority of my yearly class to the *Huszar* to take a new course, the third one now. My journal for 12 February 1864 reads, "Snow shovelled, and then deck washed."

In Italy, public opinion, stirred up by Garibaldi, was pressing for a war over Venetia. We were so convinced that one would occur that when we looked towards the opposite coast we expected to see the *Re Galantuomo* again that summer. For after the annexations

28 A strong aniseed-flavoured brandy popular in the Balkans and Greece.
29 Raimond Urbancic.
30 A schooner, the *Arethusa* was originally the *Vigilante*, and then the *Aretina*, before acquiring her definitive name in 1849. Launched in 1850, she served as a station and school vessel before being hulked and stricken in 1882. The vessel was 214 tonnes, with 11 guns and 59 crew.
31 63 ft.

of Naples, Parma, Modena and Tuscany, there were but two regions missing from the national state in order to have it form a whole, the Papal States and the Austrian possessions peopled with Italians. That the kingdom would risk an attack on the pope then seemed outside the realm of possibility, and so a war over Venetia was more certainly expected. In the meantime the Danish war broke out.

4

To the start of the German-Danish War of 1864

I doubt that more than a tenth of the officers were interested why we were fighting Denmark, and above all why this was being done allied with Prussia, and none of the men had any idea. Decrees, addresses and orders about the Holstein duchies made no impression on Venetian and Dalmatian sailors, just as Hungarian and Polish infantrymen had of necessity to be pretty indifferent. That for what Germany was holding its breath was for us nothing more than a happy event and a new war somewhere distant, a fantastic adventure which excited us.

Pola still slumbered in its apathetic desolation, among the rocks the "string quartet" had piled about the fleet. As always, the white towers of the forts were untouched and alone on the green of the hills, and no extraordinary orders affected the land garrison. But in the navy there was discussion of the rumour that a squadron was to go to the North Sea. Just the mention of such a distant sea was enough to cause amazement, for since the *Novara* had returned from her already legendary voyage around the world, no Austrian warship had left the Mediterranean, and we midshipmen who had seen Athens were considered globetrotters.

At the same time there emerged the first reports about the combats on the Eider[1] and the appointment of pilots for the North Sea, and eventually you came to believe that something was going to happen which the day before had been attacked as impossible. The long-exercised system of saving and cancelling, combined with a distaste for administrative matters, had been turned topsy-turvy. While grass literally grew in the arsenal and the temporarily disarmed ships which were to go now had to be freed of a weight of seaweed and barnacles, there were problems every second, and while the hastily assembled and augmented crews were instructed in a comical sort of way about the guns, whose simple construction had been the sole reason for their not being destroyed, so now also could the officers overcome their hatred of pen and ink. Thus, for example, one captain swore about the bad luck which had caused him to be condemned to such slavish duties away from his bridge, but in meeting this requirement he regularly stranded himself halfway from the office in the Café Gaudenz. There he stayed all morning, and if his adjutant came and tried to coax him into signing some documents he offered the most outraged resistance. "Listen, Mister," he would shout, "don't disturb my private affairs!" But then he would say appeasingly, "Sit down and be so good as to drink a couple of lemonades." Lemonade was for him the punch, the spirits of the Gaudenz, in which he drowned his troubles with pen and ink.

---

1 In the opening phases of the conflict, Prussian and Austrian troops pushed the Danes off the line of the Eider River, the southern boundary of the Danish province of Holstein.

In such conditions in 1864 it was believed a whole number of ships had to be made ready for sea. Tegetthoff, commanding the *Schwarzenberg* and *Seehund*[2] in the Levant, was well ahead of the others. He was ordered to leave for the North Sea, and as soon as he received the order he at once left the Mediterranean without consulting Pola, intending to join the frigate *Radetzky*,[3] which left Pola at the same time to break the Danish blockade of the mouth of the Elbe. The other vessels arrived slowly, one by one, up to the end of April in the harbour of Brest,[4] as their states would permit, along the way visiting a number of other harbours and having their voyages interrupted by the most unpleasant episodes as a result of the miseries of mobilization. During the latter period, on his return from the arsenal a dashing midshipman reported to the first lieutenant that he had seen to his ship's needs and had "brought with him" an extra 50 *Klafter*[5] of three-inch[6] cable without the officials knowing. Now and then you heard doubts that the armoured vessels could not take to the ocean. Moreover, during that period the commander of *Don Juan d'Austria*[7] had such a bitter quarrel with the builder[8] of this flatiron that he requested the confident expert accompany him on the voyage. Only when water poured in during a storm in the Bay of Biscay and nearly sank the ship did the builder change his mind. In short, it was a good thing no Danes were cruising in the Mediterranean or south of England, for our ships were in no way battleworthy. The only thing they did do at the start was to take two enemy merchantmen, the money from their sale being distributed among the squadron a month later. Even though I had seen nothing of the unfortunate vessels, I received two gulden seventy-six kreuzer prize money, the amount for someone of my rank. One of the Danish captains, who were held prisoner in Pola, committed suicide from grief.

The imperial fleet therefore moved to Brest one by one, beset with constant problems, while the north German press raged against it, speaking of snails and travelling in single file. But we *Saida* midshipmen were on the *Huszar* in Venice, hearing now and then about the misery in Pola, and eventually we lost all hope of being transferred to a departing ship. The first lieutenant of the *Huszar* was Weyprecht,[9] later the Arctic explorer. He was a good-natured man, always buried in his scientific research, and he allowed his charges the greatest freedom. In our despair we took to gambling. Since the brig was tied up opposite

2   A screw-propellor gunboat launched in 1861, the *Seehund* was 852 tonnes, with 4 guns and 139 crew. As Rottauscher later relates, she was heavily damaged on passage to the North Sea, but she was at Lissa. In 1876 she became a torpedo school tender and in 1887 a coal lighter. The *Reka*, *Streiter* and *Wall* were the others of this class.

3   A screw frigate launched in 1854, the *Radetzky* displaced 2 198 tonnes, had 41 guns and a crew of 412. Rebuilt several times over her career, in February 1869 she blew up with heavy loss of life off Lissa when a powder magazine exploded.

4   In fact, the harbour of Cherbourg, France, and not Brest.

5   An archaic measurement equal to 1.9 m or 6.2 ft; therefore 95 m or 310 ft.

6   The Viennese inch was practically equal to imperial measurement, so also 7.5 cm.

7   The *Don Juan d'Austria* was the sole ironclad sent to the North Sea. Launched in 1862, she was 3 588 tonnes, with 14 guns and 386 men. Having been rebuilt in 1874–76 and 1896, she was not finally stricken in 1904. She was sister ship to the *Kaiser Max* and *Prinz Eugen*. Her captain in 1864 was Alois Pokorny (1826–98), a distinguished officer who was present at Lissa and later rose to become an admiral.

8   Joseph Ritter von Romako (born 1828), who as chief designer of Austrian naval vessels between 1859 and 1882 was responsible for all the earliest Austrian ironclads and quite a few more.

9   Karl Weyprecht (1838–81). Weyprecht, who took command of the ironclad *Drache* at Lissa on the death of her captain, travelled to the Arctic islands of Novaya Zemlya in 1871 on a scientific voyage, and he was also joint leader of an Austrian Arctic expedition from 1872–74 which discovered the group of islands named Franz Josef Land by the Austrians.

the Riva degli Schiavoni,[10] in the midst of painted poles and gondolas, it was but a few paces to the best-known gaming house of the time in Venice, the Café Quadri,[11] under the residence of the imperial representative. There in the evenings, under flickering lights, there gathered around the small tables the white and brown coats of army officers,[12] and the clinking of the silver had a demonic effect on us, we who barely knew it. You lived more splendidly in black-and-yellow Italy than at home. Pressing between the gamblers were rouged dolls in colourful crinoline dresses, looking about, cigarettes between their lips, one hand on their hips and the other around the shoulder of a lucky gambler. Cyprus wine or massagram, a pungent mix of corn brandy, coffee and sugar, were served. Every evening the midshipmen of the *Huszar* formed a limited stock company, at whose head was a certain Arlech.[13] He never touched a card without it being a good one – it was if he had been inspired by the devil. We entrusted our meagre capital to him, and nearly every time he brought back forty to sixty *Quatrini*,[14] which were consumed in the 'Buon pastore' restaurant.

Confusing news reached us of Tegetthoff's fate. British public opinion was outraged by the rumour that Austria meant to intrude warships into the waters which Britain had for centuries considered exclusively her own, and this outrage knew no bounds when the commodore and his Levant squadron did indeed hasten north ahead of all others and pass the holy shores. Once we read in a British newspaper, "Yesterday three Austrian warships entered our waters to wild growling" – the men's hurrahs as they reached the Straits of Dover – "how long are we going to look idly on?" Then we heard of the sad fate of the *Seehund*, which had gone to Sheerness to coal.[15] The English pilot had deliberately caused her heavy damage and had fled to the shore. Now the ship lay in Texel, and in her place two Prussian gunboats and a paddle-steamer had sailed with the *Schwarzenberg* and *Radetzky* to battle the blockading fleet.

And ever more we heard that in Pola that every item of material was in short supply and that to hand had been ruined by time; how ships put to sea one at a time and soon thereafter had to run into foreign ports for urgent repairs. If we heard that we became sullenly enraged and went deeper at the hazard tables with the gold swordknots, thinking of nothing else than that we could not let our youth slip idly by in Venice. A soft early spring announced itself through the city. All was filled with the smell of the sea from the lagoons, and the canals looked ever stranger thanks to the rising fog and the south wind washing the plaster with its breath. Above the roofs of the palaces, evening gradually died down with improbable colours and with clouds streaming by, looking as warm as gold. And then the midshipmen swallowed their anger and wandered through the legendary confusion of the lanes, watching the night-time crowds and moving slowly across the roofs of the Rialto. The kind local people had so thoroughly lost their taste for sea-dominating sentiments, had nothing of the stubbornness of the Lombards, produced in the charcoal

---

10 One of the better-known fashionable streets of Venice, running along the shore east of St Mark's Square.

11 Very popular, and still operating.

12 White was the standard colour coat for infantry officers, brown for that of officers of the so-called frontier infantry, from the Military Frontier, an area of varying size on the empire's southeastern border.

13 Midshipman Wenzel Arleth.

14 A *quatrini* is one-sixtieth of a Tuscan lira and in modern Italian is synonomous for an extremely small amount, so it would seem the stakes and winnings of Rottauscher and his comrades were not very large at all.

15 In fact, the damage occurred while the vessel was entering Ramsgate Harbour, not Sheerness Harbour.

fumes of turbulent Milan, nor had they the maliciousness of the Romagna, whose Austrian period had been full of assassinations and dreadful struggles. The easy-going youth of the lagoons is like the graceful curve of the gondola with every movement of the rudder, like the elegant pointed works on old facades. The night-time Venetian crowds, with which we walked slowly on the roofs of the Rialto to make them sing with us in chorus their patriotic songs, sang badly but loudly – perhaps they feared our weapons. But they were likewise quickly appeased if in thanks we asked for one of their *canzone*. We soon sat together in a cheerful company, and while our unknown companions strummed their guitars and mandolins, we heard "Venezia benedetta" or "Ninetta guarda." The water of the canals flowed by, the lights of gondolas floated under the bridges, and if young girls were among our prisoners we ceremoniously accompanied them home, they leading the way with lanterns.

In March the *Huszar* left for Trieste, and at last the midshipmen seemed to have been given a hint of relief from their idle life. For there Archduke Max had just taken the imperial crown of Mexico and an Austrian free corps was forming, and nothing filled us so much as the thought to join it. For since we had been given no chance to fight the Danes, we meant at least to fight battles in America, a thought which was so seductive, as if we would stand in a tropical landscape and chastise rebels, i.e., those who did not agree with the choice of an imperial prince. In the roads of Miramar lay a French frigate and the *Novara*, which were to bring the chosen one over the ocean, and in the town the recruiters for the volunteers were at work. But the midshipmen had no luck with this corps, to which almost all of them reported. Most, myself included, were refused because they were too young.

On a marvellous spring day,[16] both ships put to sea and set course for the ocean, surrounded by the smoke of their guns, which they had in response to the salutes. The cheers and good wishes of the people roared from the city's shores. Beside me stood an old salt. He gazed pensively at the departing *Novara*, the imperial flag at her mainmast. "You'd have to give me a lot of money before I'd take his place," he said with a nod, "I know the Mexicans," and spat.

But we midshipmen said that the great chance had finally been let slip, and unwillingly we returned to the loading drill and exercising with the sails, rolling around the northern Adriatic on the *Huszar*. Eventually we were no longer sad we were not on the ships in the North Sea. The main body of them were idle in Brest, and Tegetthoff with his two were in Cuxhaven, after the Danes broke off the blockade of the mouth of the Elbe without firing a shot. They limited themselves to hunting merchantmen in the North Sea, and the British always warned them in time before the commodore came out, one of the most splendid and much-discussed acts the Royal Navy performed on this ocean.

One day it was reported to Tegetthoff that a Dane was cruising outside the harbour. The commodore at once put to sea and sighted a frigate with no colours, which on his approach fled to the open ocean. Soon, aided by a fresh wind and leaving the slower *Radetzky* behind, the *Schwarzenberg* with sail and steam pursued the enemy closely. A long time later, the enemy vessel hove to, raised British colours and revealed herself as the frigate *Aurora*.[17] Everyone said that this manoeuvre, apart from its obvious purpose

---

16 The departure took place on 15 April 1864.
17 A wooden screw frigate completed in 1863, the *Aurora* displaced 3,500 tons and had 41 guns and 540 crew. Later a training ship, she was broken up in 1891. In 1864 the *Aurora* was guard ship off the island

of learning the speed and battle-worthiness of the Austrian vessels, had the motive of temporarily diverting Tegetthoff from a new enemy piratical voyage. In the meantime, while no laurels had been won at sea, the Düppel works had been captured for a long time, while the army under Gablenz[18] had won victory after victory. The latter was already in Jutland, and the belief that the armament of the entire fleet had been pointless had gained the upper hand.

The *Huszar* entered Pola at the beginning of May. For variety, the old "Load! Load 1–1! Uncock 3–1!" with its endless tempo, was now ordered in harbour. On the 10th, we had just eaten and were occupied with this when we saw unusual activity at the arsenal; the steamer *Triest* came out, and that at speed. We were uncertain what this meant until another midshipman rushed down from the deck, shouting the very exciting news that a gig with the adjutant of Pola's harbour admiral had come alongside. There had been a bloody battle in the North Sea, he said, with 160 killed and wounded,[19] and he counted on his fingers the number of midshipmen to go there as replacements. We thought he was playing a practical joke and were pummelling him when someone shouted my name. Electrified by a sudden feeling of joy, I ran up the stairs onto the sun-washed deck. And there really did stand the adjutant, the officers pressing about him discussing the telegram he had brought. "Pack your things," he said to me, "you're leaving this evening with a transport for Hamburg."

My first reaction was one of shock, but then I flew head over heels into the cabin, tore off my seaman's clothes and rooted out my sole frock coat. So it had really come true! The long-untested navy had fought off Heligoland! And it was really again suddenly so foregone a conclusion, so obvious that it had come to a fight, that Tegetthoff had forced and won a battle. So transparently obvious! As if in a dream, I transshipped to the *Triest* with my travelling companions, another midshipman and two officers[20] – the men came on board dragging their bags, drunk and hooting. To the noise of their poor singing and clamour, we steamed into the falling night, whose morning had been like any other, blue, sultry and calm. And then there came another such morning, this time in Triest harbour. The men were silent and tired from shouting, dragging their sacks, and people looked at us in astonishment, standing in lanes or hanging in countless numbers on the fences of the railway station, which was covered by the black smoke of our train. But inside me a feeling of happiness had awakened – it was as if chains had suddenly been torn from my body, as if I was running before a storm.

---

of Heligoland (Helgoland, Germany), then a British possession. Britain was extremely favourable to the Danes during the war with Austria and Prussia, hence Rottauscher's sarcastic comments.

18 Lieutenant General Ludwig Freiherr von Gablenz (1814–74) was commander of the Austrian corps which was sent to fight the Danes during the Second Schleswig War. His troops won some notable victories, although with fairly high casualties.

19 The action, to which Rottauscher later refers, occurred on 9 May 1864.

20 These officers would seem to have been Commander Alfred Barry (1830–1907) and Commander Maximilian von Sterneck (1829–987), sent to the North Sea to assume command of the two Austrian frigates. Both men were at Lissa as ships' captains and had distinguished later careers.

5

Journey to Cuxhaven and to Tegetthoff's squadron

I regained my balance only when I reached Vienna. My training had placed over me a halo of importance – I had been one of the better sailors and was a midshipman going to war, and I thought I had to behave as such before the enthusiastic populace by being serious and composed. I found myself won over to that degree when this suggestion slowly pressed into my inner thoughts.

My heart beat faster as, leaning out the carriage window, I made out the Kahlenberg, and the men's hoarse yelling, which had restarted shortly after we left Triest and had been kept up the entire journey, now resounded through the suburbs as well. Now no more would I beat houseowner's sons from the field in the hours of dancing or parade slowly before curtsying children; now I would no more walk along the parade grounds hanging onto my father, for now I would go into foreign lands and within a few days face the enemy.

As a result, nothing depressed me more than our reception in Vienna. There was not a trace of a crowd, still less of anyone cheering. Out of sorts, we stamped along the high road through the eastern suburbs to the transit house in two rows, the men's bags on their backs. There the men were accommodated and forbidden to leave, and the festivities were at an end. The few people we met along our march stood open-mouthed, perhaps taking our unfamiliar clothing for a carnival procession or by the bags for prisoners going to labour.

Very disgruntled, I met my father, who likewise had no expectation of my future heroic deeds and said only that the Danish prisoners had become Vienna's newest attraction and that I had to see them. The approximately 500 Danish prisoners had entered the capital shortly before, and they caused general merriment by their seriousness and slowness with which they played their games of skittles. Now they looked out the windows of the Franz Joseph Barracks at the people, who in masses gazed at them all day, and they let down small baskets, and when these were filled with love-gifts[1] drew them easily up with appreciation, as if they had the hardest work to perform. From time to time they all gravely took off their caps and bowed to the crowd without seemingly exchanging a word among themselves, and every time a hundred-fold cheer resounded. But I had seen French prisoners in 1859, and in similar circumstances, and then the barracks' windows were the same as those of a madhouse. There was kicking and shouting, hanging of arms and legs, swinging of caps and a continual "Hurrah for the Viennese!", and you were really astonished how these people could keep up this sort of behaviour for weeks without dying of exhaustion.

But the droll gravity of the Danes and their unpacking of the small baskets made no impression on me, for our men far away in the transport office were more deserving of love-gifts. And just as it was during our stay in Vienna, so it was during all the journey

---

1   German *Liebesgaben*, voluntary donations made by civilians to the military in time of war.

in Austria. The 1864 war was considered as scarcely more than a professional affair of the military and did not affect the population.

Only on the other side of the Prussian border did things change, for the war was popular in the federated German states. It was seen as the first expression of national unity since the Wars of Liberation, a relief from the decades-old darkness and quarrelling of small states. But just as before, the princes' jealousy was the only reason that our transport had to take an indirect route. Saxony and Hanover were very angry they had not been allowed to be the force opposing the Danes, and it would be better for the Austrian uniform to avoid Dresden.

It suffices to say we were drowned in a sea of enthusiasm. Singing clubs stood at every station, and behind them the crowds pressed close together, and with a swinging of flags, imposing chorales poured on us. Flowers and eatables were thrown at the sailors, who threw the flowers back, for Italians feel vegetables are uneatable, and the Slav is not much different. We arrived in Breslau[2] exhausted, the men slightly tipsy. There the excitement reached a crescendo, overtopped only by that in Hamburg. Because there was no transport office, the men had to be billeted on the citizens. Our commandant gave an impressive and menacing speech about discipline, and then the men went off with their hosts, their bags still on their backs, while we members of the staff were greeted by the officers and officials with Prussian reserve and a stiffness we did not understand because of the people's joy, and whose reason we learned only in Hamburg. We did not then suspect how little our two states were in agreement up there in Schleswig-Holstein.

While our men were being most disgracefully petted by their hosts, we crossed the city together, and there we saw things which made us pensive. A conversation between two civilians disconcerted us, a quarrel in which one of them said he wanted nothing to do with the military and the other retorted, "How would you have any chance of becoming a whole man? You've never served." He uttered the jest which threw a rare light on the joke people made in Austria about the general service in Prussia. Admittedly the king's soldiers saw our cuirassiers, our gold-bedecked lancers, our frontiersmen with their gigantic moustaches, differently, but then they saw only good formations. We soon saw that our belief that one could not make a warrior out of a civilian in a short time was wrong, and another image we had of the troops likewise did not correspond. Prussia and Austria were then in southern Germany the butt of endless bad jokes, which were unfortunately believed. People were convinced that a Prussian would die of hunger and typhus on principle, that every Prussian wore a monocle, that a lieutenant of the Guards was just as *Fliegende Blätter*[3] portrayed him, a lean poltroon in tall boots crammed into a tight tunic, his spiked helmet over his ears, swinging the cord of his monocle around his index finger. Another caricature was of nine such men sitting in a restaurant with nine glasses, a bottle of water and a buttered roll. Incidentally, in 1870 the French caricatures were the exact opposite, fat-bellied suburban citizens, a metre-long pipe in their mouths and house caps on their heads, going to war.

We therefore imagined all Prussian officers and soldiers to be variations on these starvelings; they seemed harmless braggarts, and we were amazed at finding it was just the opposite and meeting cold, serious men. Moreover, we saw a characteristic Prussian scene when we were invited to watch a company drill. As the crowd pressed around the

---

2   Now Wrocław, Poland.
3   Then one of the better-known comic papers of southern Germany.

Austrians as they walked, threatening to hinder the movement of the troops, the captain waved to his drummers, who in a moment chased away the people, making their sticks dance on their heads. This proceeding made so very disagreeable an impression on us that we thought Prussia was every inch a militarized state and very dangerous.

But the men were little lost in such thoughts, gulping to the full the freedom of being billetted. Dragged by their hosts, who liked to show off their foreign guests, from one beer garden to another, they were the opposite of a well-managed transport, hanging drunkenly from any friendly shoulder and embracing men, women and children countless times and being embraced in turn. Weaving through the night-time streets with a constant crowd of admirers, they yelled out as if the world had to hear them, "All Germany will become one," the first German song and the first German words they had learned in their lives. And soon "All Germany" and "Schleswig-Holstein sea-surrounded" were on our journey the way in which our Venetians and Slavs got tremendous amounts of free beer at every station, for the trick worked like a magic wand in Frankfurt an der Oder and Berlin – everywhere the reaction was the same.

When we finally arrived at the Alster basin[4] to await our billetting tickets, the reception surpassed even that of Breslau. The men stood in a long row facing a magnificent hotel, their bags in front of them, in constant danger of being knocked into the water by the rejoicing crowd which pressed up to them. And now, now that they were again in sight of dreadful discipline, they meant to give themselves up again to totally insane celebration. As the Austrian non-commissioned officers arrived to rescue us, the men furthest down the line, made more excited by the glasses of beer thrust at them, began to sing softly, "All Germany" so as to get more and more. The non-commissioned officers tried to distribute the tickets, but the men, full of scorn for these land-rats, tore them from the hands of the sergeant majors and sergeants and in a twinkling threw themselves into the crowds, which dragged them off in wild confusion. A stream of men forced itself singing and shouting through Altona's narrow lanes, and over their heads you saw Marco and Giovanni sitting on people's shoulders, swinging their caps and bawling, "Long live Germany!" Everyone fought for the linen bags, 20 men at once carrying these costly items after their owners, and I thought that not one sailor would reach his assigned place, for he would be torn from the crowd by the people in the first houses he came to and dragged in as a valued trophy. Tumult reigned the whole night; the men and their hosts waved from lighted windows to the closely packed crowd, which shouted back. But there was a deeper reason for this reception than just "All Germany"; sympathy for our southern, light, friendly nature and antagonism for the reserved nature of the Prussian military, which treated civilians as dogs in the fullest sense of the word. Despite the Hanseatics having the same north German blood as the Prussians and thus being closer to them than the Austrians, in spite of that they ever more sought the friendship of the Prussians' rivals. Moreover, strange to say, the other side paid attention even to our uniform, as is shown by the following anecdote. A well-to-do youth left the hubbub and tried to insinuate himself with two Prussian lieutenants, who were coldly watching the scene. "What poor, plain greatcoats these Austrians have," he said. One of the lieutenants said, "That's true, but a soldier in even a shabby coat will always be worth more than a piece of shit in a fur coat like you."

The next morning I stood on the pier, counting the men as they arrived. Although the inhabitants handed over their sadly scattered guests most scrupulously, the atmosphere

---

4   A part of Hamburg, Germany, then an independent state.

was one of general merriment, and the embracing and tearful leave-takings were not easy. Moreover, I was taken for one of the heroes of Heligoland, and people pressed about me asking questions, only in the end to see by my surly expression that I would not say a word. It was lucky for me that a Prussian sailor from the *Adler*[5] was not far away, for people now gathered around him. "Well now," he shouted, "we fired a broadside and clipped the ears of the *Niels Juel*,[6] and she turned to starboard. Good appetite! There she got into the soup. Then the *Blitz* fired and hit her ribs with a twenty-four-pounder shot, while the *Basilisk*,[7] nothing loath, hit her in the bow." That was his version of events, one believed across northern Germany. But it should be noted that on Tegetthoff's orders the Prussian vessels had to halt out of range of the Danes because they were of extremely weak build.[8]

At last we set off, and to the cheers of the merchantmen we passed down the Elbe. A light rain fell, but despite that the men rejoiced in the frosty, unaccustomed weather, saying to a man that Germany and war were the finest things on earth. It also seemed that way to me. Finally we lay alongside our frigates in Cuxhaven, and then all of a sudden the seriousness of battle leaped into view before me.

---

5   The *Preussischer Adler*, to give the full name, was a paddle-steamer built in 1846/47 and requisitioned for the Prussian navy in 1868. At 1 171 tonnes, 4 guns and 100 crew, she took part in the 1864 war, and then in 1868 became the royal yacht before being stricken in 1877.
6   The *Niels Juel* propellor frigate had been launched in 1855, and displaced 2 320 tonnes with 42 guns. She took moderate damage in the action off Heligoland.
7   The *Blitz* and *Basilisk* were two gunboats of the *Camäleon* class, launched in the early 1860s. At 422 tonnes, 3 guns and 71 crew, they represented an important part of the Prussian navy in 1864. However, as Rottauscher later remarks, they were not good seaboats, rolling severely in even a moderate sea and being very wet inside. The *Blitz* was stricken in 1876 and broken up two years later, the *Basilisk* stricken in 1875 and broken up some time after 1900.
8   Rottauscher is quite correct; the Prussian gunboats took no part at all in the action.

6

Among the victors of Heligoland

On the *Radetzky*, to whose staff I was transferred, repairs were in full swing. Here and there it was still possible to see the sea through a shot hole, for the vessel had taken a total of 51 hits to her port side. In the pulleys there hung a crushed mass of wood, a totally destroyed boat, and a breach yawned in the side close to the bow. There exploded the shell which had torn to pieces my predecessor, Midshipman Bielsky. This hero had been badly wounded and was dragging himself through the gun deck leaning on his sabre. Loss of blood eventually forced him to crawl, but he was still cheering on the men when the shot tore through the planking and buried the twitching youth in fire, smoke and a hail of iron.

The men became quiet, and I too became thoughtful when the arms of those killed were distributed among them. According to the nature of the boarding parties, some received rifles and bayonets, others pistols and heavy boarding sabres, whose bulky white guards had protected the hands of men who had died only a few days ago.

Midshipman Schönberger[1] came on board and invited me to have a drink with him on the *Schwarzenberg*. This 16-year-old, who for his bravery had been awarded the gold medal,[2] was still deaf in one ear from the explosion of a shell nearby, and all the right side of his face was still singed. He said how before the battle the men had knelt to pray beside their guns. As the chaplain in full vestments went through the gun decks and the men crossed themselves, they laid their large hands on the guards of their sabres and cast furtive, curious glances at the sea and the approaching Danes. The mood on board had been almost wild, and it climbed accordingly when the first enemy shots fell short. Soon thereafter a shell came through a gunport and exploded beneath a gun, and a dazzling flash lit the gun deck; all the crew was killed, and the barrel fell to the deck almost as if it had been alive, showering a spray of splinters as it crashed down. The latter became the most dangerous thing in the battle as it developed – they caused dreadful wounds and extraordinary incidents. One of them, for example, impaled an officer's cap on his head, and then when the Danes turned away a sailor suddenly leaped high into the air, and with ghastly dance steps skipped through the battery. Since no wound was to be seen, people thought he had gone mad, something not unknown in battles. But when he fell with a frightful shriek and died he was closely examined, and it was found that his corpse bore no other mark than a thin splinter, which had penetrated his spinal cord.

I had one thought as I stepped on board the *Schwarzenberg* – how had it been possible that everyone had not been killed or wounded? The destruction on the *Radetzky* was as nothing compared to that on the flagship, on which the Danes had concentrated their

---

1 Richard Schönberger.
2 The Austrian army and navy had three sorts of medals for other ranks. The highest, the Gold Medal for Bravery, carried with it double pay while its owner was on active service. The other two were the large and the small Silver Medal for Bravery.

fire.[3] It was if they had contrived to direct precision fire on a target. The white battery stripes[4] were dotted with holes, the stump of the burned foremast stood forlornly, and the front part of the ship was half charred. There a falling piece of tackle had buried a rifled deck gun and its crew in flames, and you could still smell the unpleasant odour of the blackened wooden fittings caused by the fine rain. As you walked, you crackled over scorched planks. But most dreadful was the devastation on the inboard side. Everywhere you saw the effects of exploding shells; arm-long jagged pieces of wood had been torn from the planking; beams were ploughed up, and pieces of iron had been warped as if by a giant fist. During the bombardment of Sevastopol[5] one bomb exploding on a British battleship had caused such panic among the men of the battery that they had fled to the paddle-steamer which was alongside towing the warship. I mention this because no fewer than five shells exploded in a battery on *Schwarzenberg*, but the men nevertheless held firm to their guns, even if they were made very uneasy, and because I saw that at one point the ship's side had been torn up for eight metres[6] in such a manner as to lay bare her frame. The frigate lost nearly one-quarter of her crew within an hour. The Elbe pilots had been brave, and the one on the *Radetzky* did not leave the commander for a second, even though the bridge was then the most dangerous place on the ship.

To close this action, I will note the political importance of this bloodily bought victory. Denmark had been beaten on land by Austria and Prussia, and her sole hope was her fleet – so long as it was intact it could cause immense damage to German commerce and had done so already in abundance. But after Heligoland, the Danish fleet was no longer fit, and the Danes, robbed of their last support and forced onto the defensive on sea as on land, saw themselves necessitated to conclude an armistice, which was agreed to shortly after this battle.[7]

Both frigates were brightly lit by day and night, and the hammers of the civilian workers pounded away as we were given our first instructions, which were based on the experiences of the battle, and we were also exercised in the use of splinter nets for the first time. During all this we were badgered by visitors and journalists seeking news of the battle. Plausible and implausible accounts were spread by newspapers with a sort of greed, to the extent that one day we decided to show the gullibility of public opinion by writing the following letter:

> My name is Johannes Müller, born in Flensburg and forced to serve on the *Sjaland*.[8] At Heligoland we had 80 killed, the engine badly damaged and the steering mechanism shot to pieces. I tell you this because there is no other way the real amount of the

---

3   The *Schwarzenberg* received between 70 and 80 hits, which killed 31 men, badly wounded another 50 and lightly wounded some 23 more.

4   The side of the ship where the gunports were was marked by white stripes.

5   During the Crimean War, on 17 October 1854 the Anglo-French fleet bombarded the Russian port of Sevastopol (now in Ukraine) to support a bombardment from the land side, but the shelling was largely ineffective and the fleets took some notable losses.

6   25 ft

7   A rather doubtful assertion, since the Danish fleet also had an armoured monitor, *Rolf Krake*, a battleship, *Skjold*, and two armoured frigates, *Peder Skram* and *Dannebrog*, which would have made mincemeat of the Austrian frigatesThe armistice of which Rottauscher speaks took effect on 12 May 1864, as was worked out by the London Conference of the great powers and Denmark.

8   Properly *Sjælland*, one of the Danish frigates which took part in the battleLaunched in 1858, she displaced 2 320 tonnes and had 42 guns.

Danish losses can arrive in Germany. My parents are carters; greet them from their son!

We sealed this letter in a bottle and threw it overboard. A Hanoverian fisherman found it at the mouth of the Weser, and three days later Johannes Müller's letter was presented as an authentic account in the papers of northern Germany, discussed by experts and made the basis of leading articles. The best thing was that the fisherman got 100 thalers from the government, but this disturbed us to such a degree we agreed to keep absolute silence about the case. Only today, 50 years on, I think I may draw aside the curtain from Müller's tale of woe without feeling uneasy.

There was endless jubilation in Cusnase and Risibisi, as our sailors called Cuxhaven and Ritzenbüttel, and it did not let up during this period. Not a day went by without vistors from all parts of Germany. They arrived in broad-beamed coastal vessels, paying respectful homage to the last corner of the memorials to the newly awakened national unity, sanctified by shells and flames. On land, one celebration lit by Chinese and storm lanterns succeeded another – there were banquets for the officers and dances for the sailors. Midshipman Schönberger said our frigate's first reception had been totally different. For then the dubious conception of the horrors of Magdeburg,[9] of the imperials and especially of the Croats in *Wallenstein's camp*[10] haunted all their heads. Others, as Schiller had thought they might, had been influenced by the scene as a moral preparation, and had to entail a flight from any womanish fuss. Now everything had changed: the sounds of the "Radetzky March"[11] pealed continuously through the garland-bedecked halls, the sailors agreed most easily by means of sign language with the blonde, melancholy maidens, and we officers, looking down from the gallery and drinking, took pleasure in them and the perfumed notes sent to us by the most gracious women of country seats. They hung about even the youngest midshipmen; even those who were half children did not escape. Indeed, those with black bandages around their foreheads or with their arms in slings had particularly to suffer on in the fullest sense on eagerly outstretched arms. However, there was too much admiration and love, and many heroes preferred silent pralines or nut cakes.

"Mummy's coming" was a catchphrase in the squadron; the sailors termed any officer on duty or inspecting mummy, for "mummy's coming" was the warning call to their girls. When I think back, many female hearts were brutally trampled; sentimentality was rewarded with realism, enrapturement with hard knocks.

In our free time we read love letters on the deck. A circle of men would squat around a petty officer, who would sit on an overturned water cask, pipe in mouth, and translate the letters seriously with a lack of German, so giving cause for blame or approval of the writer. Now a melancholy passage was barely acknowledged, the maiden who had conceived it loudly condemned as robbing a soul of peace, and there was horror on the faces of the superstitious men. Some days it was certain that all German girls had the evil eye. What the men got from this conviction I do not know.

---

9   During the Thirty Years' War in the 17th century, the north German city of Magdeburg had been sacked and almost all burned to the ground by the emperor of Austria's forces.

10   A renowned three-part poem by Friedrich Schiller (1759–1805), one of Germany's most famous poets, which detailed the events of the Thirty Years' War.

11   A very favourite Austrian army march composed by the famous Austrian composer Johann Strauss the elder (1804–49).

In short, our time in Cuxhaven was one of pure delight. Only two things were unpleasant, the Elbe and the Prussians. We had to fight hard against the unaccustomed river current and the speed with which the Elbe poured its waters into the sea at ebb tide, and this caused the most disagreeable incidents. Once I was duty midshipman and had to go to meet some officers on shore. A strong northwest wind had forced the Elbe upstream, and just as we descended from the gangway to return to the ship, the dreadful pull of the current began. We first touched upwards on the shore so as to fall down at an angle and reach the *Radetzky*. There, by ill luck, a boat was hanging from the back boom, and in the darkness we only saw it shortly before it emerged before us. All of us thought that we must invariably capsize, but as we bounced off it our boat raised it into the air, and it fell on us like a horse, breaking the ribs of two men and hitting Midshipman Henneberg,[12] who was sitting next to me, on the shoulder and knocking him into the river. Then the current tore us away from the frigate, from which lifelines were thrown to us. People yelled; lights showed above here and there, and it was only with difficulty that the already very exhausted midshipman could succeed in dragging himself into the boat. We worked with the strength born of desperation and only after some hard work came alongside once more. A second such incident occurred when a visitor slipped off the companionway as he was climbing it and disappeared into the river before anyone could come to his aid. Not a trace remained of him, no one knew his name or learned it later, and his top hat swam on its lonely way down to the open sea.

If this was sinister enough, and with many other incidents disturbed our celebrations so that you never knew if you would return on board safe and sound, so there was also between ourselves and our allies an unspoken but extremely acute antagonism. Moreover, it was increased by Austrian army officers who spent their leave in Cuxhaven during the period of the armistice concluded soon after Heligoland[13]. The officers of the Prussian ships avoided us and we them, and if we did meet we exchanged greetings in a formal manner. The idea of a coming war was already in the air; it was clear to everyone that the concept of equal rights would not last for ever, and for no one was the question of supremacy more burning than for those who had fought Denmark together and had seen for themselves the inadequacy of the system. While the captain of the Hamburg company was numbered among our truest boon companions, while chorus singers and the people indefatigably repeated the "Radetzky March" and the national anthem,[14] the Prussians held coolly aloof. This situation indeed caused comic scenes, such as the one in which a one of our petty officers, pretty well flushed with drink, stood up from his table and tried with a full heart to express his patriotism. Staggering along, he eventually landed up at a mate from the *Adler* and pressed him very urgently to drink the pledge of brotherhood.[15] When the latter, who sat alone in front of his beer mug, coldly rapped out "No," our sentimental one began his poetic rapture with a drunk's usual confused train of thought. In tears, he shouted, "If my emperor calls, if my emperor calls, I'll die for him, I'll gladly let myself be shot for him!" The Prussian endured this monologue for quite a while, but then he addressed the other with all the coldness at his command. "Why are

12   In fact Sub Lieutenant Edmund Ritter von Henneberg.
13   Notwithstanding the armistice, both sides were intransigent about a final peace settlement, and on 25 June hostilities broke out afresh and lasted until 20 July, when the definitive armistice was arranged.
14   The Austrian national anthem at this period was "God preserve Franz the emperor," composed by the celebrated Joseph Haydn (1732–1809)The Germans later appropriated its tune for *Deutschland über alles*.
15   A German drinking custom in which people link arms and pledge brotherhood to one another.

you going on like this to me?," he asked, "to let yourself be shot if it pleases you – well, that's your look-out! I'll never think of death as something pleasing!" And with that he took his mug and left the astonished Austrian sitting.

The army officers told us again about the unbearable arrogance, tedious correctness and megalomania of our allies. But more dangerous were the jokes they cracked about the Prussian army. They had pretty nearly one belief about it: the men looked good and the officers were dashing, but the Prussian way of making war lacked soldierly qualities. They did not subscribe to our heroic principle of assaulting whenever we could, and without this principle war would be completely lacking in poetry. They would literally say, "You know, they do things in a really funny way. First they go left, and then they go right, and last of all they go to the right rear." Only a few expressed different views.

So during the time of the armistice sneering remarks flew by on one side and celebrations on the other. We had no great desire for Denmark to give in, and our wish was granted. Tegetthoff came on board, accompanied by a commodore, and he inspected the repairs to the last detail. Then he addressed the assembled crew, praising their bravery in the action at Heligoland in the most flattering manner and speaking of his hope for new feats of arms. The admiral stood close by the capstan, his arms crossed. He had about him an eternal calm, nothing of slovenliness or agitation as has been represented.

I also recall an anecdote from this time which is characteristic of him. As the *Schwarzenberg* was running into Cuxhaven, the smoke of her burning wounds still rising, the officers rowing for Tegetthoff conveyed their congratulations. He was at first quite taken aback and reserved, but then his thirst for action won through and he broke out in bitter laughter. "Before," he called in his rough manner, gesturing to the stump of the mast, "you congratulate me, gentlemen, please have a look at the shitty mess we've made forward."

The armistice ended without peace having been concluded. As is known from reliable sources, the Danes had made their three damaged vessels battle-ready once more, their ironclad *Dannebrog*[16] and two gunboats were cruising in the Sound, and we had to be ready to oppose a sudden twofold superiority. Thus on 24 June, *Schwarzenberg*, *Radetzky* and two Prussian gunboats put to sea so as to join the other ships, which were off Texel.

---

16   The *Dannebrog* was a battleship launched in 1850 and converted to an armoured frigate in 1863She was quite powerful, at 3 075 tonnes and 16 guns.

7

Looking for the Danes. The operation against Sylt. Homecoming

For the first time in my life I was on a ship at sea in the middle of a war, and that had a pretty powerful effect on my imagination, all the more because the weather was right for that sort of thing. A storm from the southwest let the waves drive thunderously against the high-decked frigate; rattling, they beat against the closed gunports. The cannon creaked against their restraining tackle, and rainbow after rainbow soared over us. I looked out at the sea, which one moment was overhung with clouds and the next brightly lit, experiencing the unkind, unaccustomed behaviour of the yellow, northern, sea to the fullest. All of us were quite used to a southern blue and a brilliant sun.

Because the *Schwarzenberg* had a more powerful engine, she was running ahead of us, and we could follow only with difficulty, and then last the two Prussians. It was truly bad to see how the small gunboats fought the sea, they often completely disappearing in the breaking mountains of water, and then shooting out from them to hasten feebly and despairingly after us. It would have been better for them to have been destroyed before they had been made answerable for their inaccessibility. I looked over with my glass, but there was no signal to request they be allowed to run into port, only wave after wave rolling over the Prussians' low decks and the foam mingling with the black smoke from their funnels. Finally the *Schwarzenberg* ordered the *Blitz* and *Basilisk* to bear away for the Weser. The two boats showed their sterns in a pitiable manner and hastened away through the low-sweeping clouds.

We were now not hampered by considerations of thoughtfulness, and for some time we held our original course, but then Tegetthoff hoisted a signal for us to make ready to be towed. With great difficulty the *Schwarzenberg* lowered a boat, and it took us in tow with just as much difficulty. Soon it steered for the side of the flagship, which bobbed about deep into the ocean like a monstrous wooden mountain. Then, just as the boat was dangling over the water from the tackles, the *Schwarzenberg* rolled heavily. It was as if the crane had shot the little boat far out into the ocean. A sailor was flung out into the waves like a puppet, hit the sloping side of the frigate and slid off into the waves with the recoil, to be gobbled up by the raging sea without a hope of being rescued.

Tegetthoff now towed us for some time. The two vessels dragged violently, giants chained together, and then with a crack the hawser split, part of it whipping back with a bang and writhing across our deck like an angry snake. It was now impossible to keep up with the more powerful *Schwarzenberg*. The admiral ordered us to turn back for Cuxhaven and stay there until better weather and continued on alone. In such a storm there was nothing to fear from the Danes.

As we bore away, the *Radetzky* rolled so dreadfully many times that everyone thought she would by and by capsize. The cannonballs fell from their racks and flew through the batteries, the guns tore and groaned at their sea moorings, while mountains of water slammed against the ship's side as if they wanted to force their way in. Another sailor fell overboard, the second in an hour, and the shrill, frightful cry of "Man overboard!", the warning squall of the bosun's pipe and the noise of the engine-room telegraph ran through my dreams all night.

The *Radetzky* stayed in Cuxhaven until the 26th, then recommencing her journey. At first we had better weather, but soon a new storm arose. But we had to go on, for we thought that in a better sea we would encounter the entire Danish fleet; we could not flee upriver like the gunboats, which would have had nothing edifying in that. We reached Texel in an awfully banged-about condition.

Despite our misgivings that we could not take on a pilot in such severe weather, we finally had to tack, and a cutter sailed towards us. As if she wanted to demonstrate the reputation of Dutchmen as outstanding seamen, she at once sent a jolly boat with two men, and a few moments later there stood on our deck a corpulent, pleasant gentleman in a top hat who greeted us with a laugh, as if he was entering a tearoom. He replied to our passionate questions about the squadron by assuring us that the Austrians were enjoying themselves excellently, a piece of news which reassured us very much.

The following ships lay before Texel: the ironclad *Don Juan d'Austria*, the battleship *Kaiser*,[1] the frigate *Schwarzenberg*, the corvette *Erzherzog Friedrich*,[2] the gunboats *Seehund* and *Wal* and the paddle-steamer *Elisabeth*.[3] They were commanded by Rear Admiral von Wüllerstorff,[4] a highly educated scientific man who had commanded the *Novara*'s voyage of discovery. Functioning as his flag captain was his closest friend, Baron Pöck,[5]

---

1   Built between 1855 and 1862, the *Kaiser* was one of the last, if not the last, wooden battleships constructed in the world. Steam-powered, of 5 194 tonnes with 90 officers and 904 crewmen, she was present at Lissa, taking very heavy damage and casualties but acquitting herself splendidly. Between 1869 and 1874 she was rebuilt as an armoured casemate ship, and then modernized between 1880 and 1882 before being hulked in 1902. She was last heard of in 1920.

2   Launched in 1857, the *Erzherzog Friedrich* frigate was converted to screw propulsion two years later. At 1 570 tonnes, 22 guns and 294 crew, she was also present at Lissa. Rebuilt between 1877 and 1880, the frigate was later a training ship which made several cruises around the world. She was broken up between 1897 and 1899.

3   The *Kaiserin Elisabeth*, to give her full name, was a paddle-steamer launched in 1854. She was intended as a scout, and at 1 570 tonnes had 4 guns and 166 crewmen. She too was present at Lissa as a signal repeater for the ironclads, miraculously surviving despite being repeatedly singled out by the Italian behemoths. In 1882 she became a torpedo-boat tender and tug and in 1892 was hulked.

4   Bernhard Freiherr von Wüllerstorff und Urbair (1816–83) entered the Austrian navy in 1833. As captain of the *Novara*, he commanded her during her three-year (1856–59) voyage around the world which collected a mass of valuable scientific data and specimens. In 1861 Wüllerstorff was created a rear admiral, and in March 1864 he was made head of the squadron which was to go to the North Sea to support operations against the Danes. However, as Rottauscher remarks, before Wüllerstorff could arrive Tegetthoff had fought the only major action, and there was nothing for the rest of the squadron to do. Wüllerstorff was subject to much criticism for his supposed inaction, as Rottauscher remarks probably unfairly, and he was placed on the inactive list. From 1865 to 1867 he was minister for trade and commerce, returning briefly to service in the latter year before retiring as a vice admiral in 1869.

5   Friedrich Freiherr von Pöck (Pöckh) (1825–84) entered the Austrian navy in 1843 and was promoted captain in July 1861. As Rottauscher notes, he had been second in command to Wüllerstorff when the latter commanded the *Novara* on her voyage of circumnavigation. In February 1864 he was made captain of the *Kaiser* and flag captain to Wüllerstorff, but like him did not see action in the Danish war. During

his immediate subordinate on the *Novara* as well. The latter was what was called an iron head and no warrior, and despite his greater maritime talents, nothing pained him so much as to twice have his request to transfer to the cavalry turned down by His Majesty. As we heard, the victor had been received with no special amiability by these two. The thorn of Heligoland sat in the hearts of these ambitious men; moreover, by Tegetthoff's appointment as rear admiral he had been put over the head of Pöck, who was senior in rank as a captain.[6] Such human failings may seem petty at first sight and unworthy of anyone. But even so, a much younger officer had had the good fortune to precede the elite of the squadron and beat the enemy. Neither Pöck nor Wüllerstorff bore any blame for the desperate conditions, caused only by the system of past years, but they had been condemned for their caution and for their diligent but thankless task of silently arming the squadron. But now the squadron had ripened into a force to be reckoned with, as much for its internal value as for the importance it presented to the outside world. Now of course it could make something of a figure, but in the meantime another man had won a victory, and his name outshone those of his superiors, while the quiet labours of the latter were remembered by no one. And as happens many times in life, which raises humour to the point of grotesqueness, so it was also two years later that this other, this much younger officer, forced himself into the history of the world with a fleet whose nucleus Wüllerstorff had tempered before Texel and who had drilled its seamen. We on the *Radetzky* saw assembled such well-drilled vessels, such as had never been beheld under the imperial flag in such numbers. The poor relations between the commanders were scarcely visible to the outside world; we knew that Tegetthoff was enough of a man to listen to a superior in silence. Wüllerstorff burned to be able to measure himself with the enemy; in short, there was every prospect of a great naval battle. No less was the change in the way in which the Dutch behaved towards us. British public opinion raged against Austria, which was reason enough for the Dutch to value us. We were surrounded in restaurants and bars, for we guests had to be prevented from throwing our cigar stubs on the ground. This society was fanatical about cleanliness, and we already had such a bad reputation that the mere sight of a glowing cigar sufficed to cause a real commotion of small bowls to appear around and under the object. Most charming young girls with golden hair stood there earnestly, each one with her ashtray and looking at us beseechingly.

But Britain always went further, and soon I saw with my own eyes an example of this. Shortly after the squadron reunited, we left Texel and traversed the North Sea on a rigorous reconnaissance as far as the tip of Jutland, but to Wüllerstorff's wrath we did not see a single Dane, and then we returned once more to old Cuxhaven. Then there appeared a paddle-steamer of the Royal Navy. Did it come, annoyed that we had deliberately passed Heligoland under the British guns, or was it that the British now found it necessary to inspect the new squadron so as to report about it to Copenhagen? Like someone out for a walk who is gazing about him, the vessel slowly steamed down the line of Austrian warships, her officers on deck and some of them making copious notes.

When now the Briton dropped anchor close above us, in Cuxhaven there was as much indignant bitterness as on the fleet. The townspeople did what was forbidden us by the

---

the 1866 war, Pöck was naval liaison officer at the headquarters of the Austrian army in Italy and so was not at Lissa.

6   When Archduke Leopold was head of the navy, he favoured Pöck over Tegetthoff by promoting him substantive rear admiral a day before the hero of Heligoland.

laws of nations: they showed open hostility, refused to sell food, and when the British officers and men came ashore they pressed about them with so many threats and abuse that the uninvited guests thought it prudent to steam away the same evening.

Wüllerstorff, who had hoped for a real battle, now found himself in the unpleasant situation of an admiral who neither could or was allowed to come up with the enemy. The Danes lay in the mass of islands of the Sound, and for political reasons it was impossible to enter that body of water – it was feared Britain would declare war if that happened. So public opinion in Germany forced us to attack Sylt and Föhr, an operation which did not stand as the most longed-for vision in a dream. But a curious phenomenon of mass pyschology also affected the government, and with that the squadron. Since the start of hostilities, the Danish captain Hammer[7] had steadfastly maintained himself on Sylt for the best of reasons, namely that no one had seriously tried to do him harm. Now, when there was nothing left for the army to liberate and new sensations threatened not to appear, there suddenly arose a rumour that Captain Hammer was punishing the German population of the islands most brutally, taking revenge on these defenceless people for Danish defeats. The origin of this rumour, which had no basis in reality and aroused the cries of a million men, belongs to a region which often seems to border on pathological behaviour or animal pyschology. All northern Germany was suddenly bewitched by the thought that the captain was a bloodthirsty murderer who had to be neutralized or he would kill the Sylters before the conclusion of peace. Even our devoted Cuxhaveners here and there intermingled the roar of "Captain Hammer! Where is Captain Hammer?" with the sounds of the "Radetzky March" or at a celebration.

So for better or worse we had to set out to capture this dangerous man. Comprehensive measures were taken by sea and by land, for refugees had done the most they could to exaggerate the size of the Danish force. In truth, this consisted of about 150 side waiters and some cutters fitted with small crab-bars. *Schwarzenberg, Radetzky, Wal* and *Seehund*, as well as the Prussian gunboats, set off in calm weather to support the action from the water side. While the Austrian vessels took station before the entrances to the archipelago, two Prussian gunboats pushed into the shallow Wattenmeer,[8] and at the same time an Austrian rifle battalion waded over to Sylt. Our frigates lay becalmed in the smooth, clammy swell, and we could barely make out the thin streak of the small islands on the horizon. The landing parties stood ready on deck and in the batteries, naval infantry[9] in addition to the main boarding party of sailors, whose braided caps were tied tightly under their chins. The boats were ready to sail, the small landing cannon already stowed in them. So we stood like this for hour after hour, the men leaning against the rails, their rifles between their knees. The frigate continued to dip gently, first to starboard, and

---

7 Otto Christian Hammer (1822–92). Hammer became a second lieutenant in the Danish navy in 1843 and saw action during the 1848–50 conflict with the Germans over Schleswig-Holstein. Promoted lieutenant in 1851, he was made lieutenant commander in 1858, and it was with this rank (and not post captain as Rottauscher says) that he was placed in charge of the defence of the north Frisian Islands during the 1864 campaign. Hammer's knowledge and skilful use of the shifting channels enabled him to hold out until just before the end of the war. In 1889 he was created an honorary captain.

8 The local name for this arm of the North Sea between the North Frisian Islands and the coast, which derives from *Watten*, sandbanks which are visible at low tide.

9 In 1799 the Austrians raised a force of so-called naval infantry, equivalent to the marines of other fleets. Disbanded from time to time, the naval infantry was finally abolished definitely in 1868. They were used for boarding and landing parties.

then to port, mechanically raising a dripping flank from the sea. Many times one of the officers of the watch climbed to the bridge to search the islands with a telescope. After a long while we imagined we heard the dull boom of a cannon. Perhaps it was an illusion, though, for the shallow water had forced us to keep too far off the coast.

We waited until evening. The Prussian gunboats returned and signalled that the Danish garrison had surrendered. The captain had done the most sensible thing and had capitulated to a force five times his own; the ambition to be a hero was foreign to the big man. So we reluctantly disarmed and once more set course for Cuxhaven.[10]

But through all German lands there was but one cry of joy: "Hammer has been captured!" In the pubs, people sang, to the tune of the Danish war song the "Valiant Man," mocking verses on an easy-going man who his enemy had branded with the undeserved title of a warlike and bloodthirsty buccanneer.

Shortly thereafter peace was concluded, and with it our hoped-for Trafalgar was laid to rest. We rolled about in north German harbours for some time more, in Hamburg and Bremerhaven. But we were important people who had now no reason for being there, and as hard as the parting was we had to take our leave before people became sick of us. However, many of us stayed. One man who had become engaged left the service to count the coffee sacks and note the price of the tobacco of his father-in-law, a Hamburg senator; another had been overcome with longing for the coast of his homeland, the gloomy sea and the white flag with the black eagle. Some north German officers of our navy, among them my old comrade Mensing, entered Prussian service.

At last the squadron put to sea, for the south. In the end, despite the true friendships we had made, we were in a certain sence pleased to be leaving, for we had become fed up with endless parades before princes and potentates, of which there were then in Germany sufficient unto a degree, for we seemed to have become their showpieces after the peace. Once more the journey had its amusing incidents. The pilot we had shipped as a supernumary greeted the appearance of every lighthouse along the coasts of the Channel with the thunderous shout of "A light!" Now along these coasts there was a light every 10 miles.[11] But if we asked him what the light meant, he would say as seriously, "I do not know." On his account we had to endure heavy weather, and despite the fact that from political reasons British harbours were forbidden to us, we had to run into Southampton Harbour and so received the highest praise from the old sea-dog, who according to our understanding knew every part of this body of water. "Very good," he called, "but now we have to have a Southampton pilot." He was the spitting German counterpart of Garafolo.

After a voyage which brought the captain and the first lieutenant to the verge of despair, we arrived in Brest. And I, who in the jubilation had totally forgotten that a few months before I had been ready to throw myself into the Mexican adventure, learned to thank my guardian angel for having protected me from it. For although Bazaine[12] was still in North America with the French auxiliary corps, a transport ship had just brought his sick and wounded to Brest, and the sight of the men carried over the ocean was sad in the highest degree. Now I was struck by the sufferings of a war in the tropics when I

---

10 Hammer surrendered on 19 July, and the armistice began on the 20th.
11 Assuming nautical miles, 18.5 km or 11.5 miles.
12 Achille Bazaine (1811–88), then a French lieutenant general, conquered Mexico during 1863 and 1864, but he was recalled in 1867. He is principally known as commander of the major regular French army during the Franco-Prussian War.

saw these yellow, ashen faces. Moreover, the things the men said made you fear even then that Emperor Max's cause would suffer disaster.

Depressed by such forebodings, we continued our voyage. The fleet lay in Cadiz for four whole weeks, removing the sinners of the war by dismissal or imprisonment. But we with no black marks against us revelled and caroused like Landsknechts in the beautiful city, whose warmth allowed us to breathe freely and drove away the northern chill. We wandered through the blindingly white lanes, let ourselves be roasted by the sun and gazed at the dusky maidens on the overhanging balconies – it was light, air and trembling heat. Everything from my youth seems to me to be a colourful succession of pictures from a mad, marvellous dream: early spring clouds over a cool St Mark's Square, the madness of friendship in the German states, the frigate as it coaled, storms, quiet hours in the cellar of the Bremen city hall, with its massive beams, and now castanets and fandangos. But through all this there lived tremendously in us the words of a British post captain who was a friend of the victor of Heligoland. When the one-armed veteran had drawn from a circle of us, myself included, all the details of the action, he looked into his glass, which he had lowered before him, and said, "I am proud to say Tegetthoff is my friend, and you'll see, we'll hear more of him."[13]

---

13 Original in English.

8

Up to the war for Venice

In 1865 I was transferred to the guardship of Pola Harbour, the brig *Montecuccoli*, and studied for the officer's examination. For the first time I was entrusted with a command. Venetian fishermen had reported that a Trabakel[1] laden with wood had capsized in the Quarnero.[2] The port admiral gave me command of the salvage expedition, and so I went to sea in a naval bragozzo.[3] Singular as it sounds, the Austrian navy then still reckoned among its vessels bragozzi, Trabakels and pirogues. The bragozzi had a four-man crew, the Trabakels one of eight, the latter being fitted with two crabs, while the pirogues, which were exclusively employed as flat-bottomed craft on the lagoons and Mantua's swampy lake,[4] had a gun in the bow. The vessels were commanded by a cadet or a petty officer. So I put to sea, but my happiness at my first independent command did not last. The wind became stronger, and after two days of fruitless cruising the waves forced me to bear away for an eastern Istrian port, Porto di Bradó.[5] Food as well as money were at an end, and the Trabakel, if it had existed, had been wrecked for quite a long time. So I sent a man to go to Pola on foot for orders. With the country roads today, his journey would have been a pleasant, minor one, but things were different then.[6] The day, the night and another day passed before the sailor, his uniform in tatters, ragged and done in, returned with money and the news that I might enter the naval harbour. He looked just like how two deserters in Senegambia were handed over to me by French spahis.[7] Indeed, how wretched our means of communication were with the interior of the peninsula, which none of us had then crossed, proof of which was that the servant girls of the few officers' families were peasants who came to market from every outlandish region to intercept people by the first houses and sell their foodstuffs.

And when a spring snowstorm forced hundreds of snipes to descend, this bird would become for two full days a general article of food. From the port admiral to the meat-eater, their existence was based solely on snipes, as if you were not in the 19th century but in the year 1000 in a fortified German town.

Unaffected by any newly imported, womanly tomfoolery, I would stride, books under my arm, through the tumble-down gates, the narrow sidestreets grinning at the town through their curves, over the hills in the region and through the ditches in the interior circle of forts which were halfway passable. There stood a work now abandoned today, Castioni vecchi. From its white tower you could see down to the harbour and a

---

1 Italian *trabaccolo*, a small, solidly built, two-masted sailing boat much used for transporting goods around the Adriatic.
2 Kvarner, the strait between the Istrian Peninsula and the island of Cherso (Cres, Croatia).
3 A small Venetian fishing craft native to the Adriatic.
4 In fact, the extensions of the Mincio River north and south of the city of Mantua, an important Austrian fortress.
5 Budava, Croatia.
6 The distance today between Budava and Pula is only 12 km, or 7.4 miles.
7 Mounted Arab or black horsemen in regular French service.

long way along the coast. The coastline spread out bizarrely, immense claws striking into the sea and blue water lapping deeply into them. The region was characterized by small trees like cork trees and by hills covered with short, grey-green grass which looked like fabric. If you turned to look north, the outlines and jagged precipices of the karst made the horizon look exactly like how the mountains of the moon are shown in geography books. Nothing so expresses the soul of this region as when on a sunny day a wandering cloud from the sea spreads its melancholy shade over the dead-still landscape, slipping over the hills to dim the chalk-white masses like a black spot.

There above at the white tower I often lay, above me the tops of the few Scots pines a sentimental fort commandant had planted with great difficulty, turning the leaves of my books. Many times there rode by the port admiral, Baron von Bourguignon,[8] meerschaum pipe in his mouth. He was a pleasant old gentleman who had contributed not a little to improving midshipmen's conditions. Therefore he rarely neglected to address us publicly and to be friendly. That came honestly from his heart and was, incidentally, also because of a wish to find an attentive audience for his proverbial yarns. For example, he would say to me, "Let me tell you," and I must here mention at the same time that to this day a naval officer cannot be too deeply distressed by the accusation that he knows nothing about horses. "Let me tell you, once I had a jolly good experience with my thoroughbred Arabian. I was flying along at a gallop when suddenly something hit me on the shoulder. What on earth was that, I thought to myself. I galloped on, and there it was again. What the devil, no one has a faster horse than me, have they? But there was no one to be seen far and wide, for I was in the Nubian Desert. Finally I understood. What was it? The steed was running so fast he was hitting me with his hind hooves." Then the admiral would give such a crafty wink that you did not know if he was amused by deliberately telling such a whopper or if he was on the watch for the slightest twitch of the corners of your mouth and would then become angry. He was a man of honour through and through, a real model of chivalrous gentility whose sole nickname with us was the knight without fear and without reproach.[9]

Then the period of the examination approached for me. Like all other examinations, it was held at the Hydrographical Institute in Triest. In the meantime Tegetthoff, who had been cruising in the Levant, making a practical and thorough of the experiences of the Danish naval war, Tegetthoff had become president of the commission, and he was in the most awkward humour. Although I had prepared myself most thoroughly, I expected to have an unpleasant time of it when I saw candidates who had entered the hall before me slinking away with gloomy faces. Many joked with me that our reasoning itself would be taken away and gaps tested in every subject which were inaccessible to a midshipman. The discontent in Venetia had risen and our fleet had still not increased in size or type of vessels vis-à-vis the enemy's. Moreover, the construction of two ironclads, *Erzherzog Max*

---

8   Anton Michael Freiherr Bourguignon von Baumberg (1808–79). Bourgignon entered the navy in 1825 and had extensive service, rising to rear admiral in 1859. He was appointed port admiral of Pola in December 1864, and as Rottauscher later remarks was extremely active in helping outfit the fleet for sea in 1866. Bourguignon was promoted vice admiral in June 1866, and then the first Austrian full admiral in 1875. Very popular, even beloved, Bourguignon was sometimes dubbed "the god of the sea."

9   This phrase is commonly used to describe the French knight Pierre Terrail, Seigneur de Bayard (died 1534), a nobleman and a hero of numerous actions during the campaigns in Italy of the period.

and *Habsburg*,[10] was but sluggish. Without these two it was not thought we could oppose the Italian squadron. Moreover, the admiral was bored by having been removed from his exercises, and apart from that he had, to his great misfortune, different opinions from those of the other commissioners. While the latter only asked about the most minute details of rigging, tacking, bracing yards and the confusion of towing the battleship or the frigates, Tegetthoff lay sunk in his easy chair, interrupting by firing short questions about armour or engines, causing the members of the commission to lose their composure, as no less the candidates. I admitted shamefacedly I did not know the location of the standing part of the bracing yard. Perhaps I owed my pass to the admiral's decision or to the fact that I was the fourth last examined, but for all that the commissioners objected loudly while Tegetthoff nervously drummed his fingers on the tabletop. However, the drumming was not meant for me – a loud alarm would become cold silence in a moment.

Although I was still far from being allowed to sew the gold stripes of a sub lieutenant on my sleeves, I had the announcement of my pass in my pocket, and the delivery of my commission was only a matter of time. I was embarked on the gunboat *Dalmat*, which lay in Triest Harbour. However, my lucky passing of the examination had such an effect on me that I quite foolishly slipped away and walked around town for some days, sleeping in cafés. Finally the bloodhounds succeeded in capturing me, and I was arrested by a midshipman in a very formal manner and walked onto the gunboat a prisoner, to sit on a coil of rope in the hold in total darkness and meditate on my atrocious crime.

On the whole, the *Dalmat* was a happy ship. Her first lieutenant would go on land to at night slip alongside in a civilian boat, suddenly spring on deck like a corsair, and then hunt for improprieties with a panting breath. As a result, there was a continuous silent war between him and the watch. It only sufficed for one happy little ship to sail by in the darkness to draw the warning cry of "Boat ahoy!" from the sentries. Whether allowed or not, the midshipman of the watch commanded two men at the entry port, while below in the general tumult, tarot cards disappeared and lights were blown out. Many times we outwitted the first lieutenant; many times he outwitted us. Then it became known he was lurking in the shadows close by in a Trabakel until the watch became tired, and then he would suddenly shoot up. Also amusing were the exercises in boarding, the zealous direction of which was the *Dalmat*'s strong point. Once a week the afterdeck was stormed with swinging sabres and thrusting bayonets. At one of these manoeuvres I slipped and fell, sticking my sabre in my neck to such a degree that for six weeks I lay ill. Each day I feared I would be landed and sent to a hospital, a disagreeable thought because cholera was raging on shore.

In the spring of 1866 the *Dalmat* went to Pola. There, to our astonishment we were greeted by a group of workmen, who put the ship into the best possible condition. No one knew why; most of us agreed that the gunboat was destined for Kiel, and someone said a squadron was to return to the North Sea. But when repairs were over, we were ordered to go to Piraeus using sails only, and so in the end it was the same old story. To our left, the white crags accompanied us and all about us was the loneliness of the sea.

10   These vessels had been laid down in Trieste and were suffering a protracted gestation. They were completed in the nick of time for the 1866 war and took a prominent part at Lissa, *Ferdinand Max* delivering the death blow to the *Re d'Italia*. At about 5 140 tonnes, 18 guns and a crew of nearly 500, they were Austria's most modern in 1866. *Ferdinand Max* was modernized in 1880 and hulked in 1899, *Habsburg* modernized in 1877, rebuilt from 1880 to 1883, and then reduced to an accommodation ship in 1886 before being stricken and broken up in 1898.

Seagulls flew over the boat and followed it, from time to time diving into its wake like snowflakes descending from a clear sky. Both watches competed to see who could reef the sails in record time, so that according to our notes we would have been in Kiel for quite some time before we ran through the Corfu Channel for the first time. No one knew what was going on in the world, so very occupied were we with this springtime excursion and the changing of the wind, so that the greatest piece of news we had was when the commandant of the *Reka*, which was lying off Piraeus, came on board with the newly introduced distinctions of a lieutenant commander on his sleeves.[11]

As a result, we were extremely excited by the alarming news which poured over us in an endless stream! The main import was: relations with Italy and Prussia were disturbed in equal degree and we had to make ready to be recalled. The expectation which had been seen as natural for years since the continuous successes of the Italian national movement had suddenly been realized. The battle for Venetia, the last Austrian possession on the Italian peninsula, seemed about to start, the battle for the same Venice which we considered our capital after Vienna.

We had scarcely discussed this news properly when there came a telegram to the effect that we return with all six boilers heated. So now the two ships returned along the same route the *Dalmat* had rambled leisurely along under sail, the heavy black smoke of their funnels rolling over them.

We ran into Corfu to coal. Unbelievable rumours were already being spread about the town's cafés, and newspapers had put out special editions in which bloody encounters abounded, despite the fact that all was deepest peace. A Prussian corvette lay in the harbour, likewise recalled and likewise occupied in carrying out a hasty coaling. While the Corfiotes imagined they would see a duel off the island, we lay at anchor beside one another, full of suspicion. The guards challenged each other, and since there was no official news from home we had no real idea if we were still allies or already enemies. On a riding to the noontime gun, my nag threw me. I had just gathered my wits in the ditch into which I had been flung when up there trotted some Prussian officers, including one who had served with me at one time. Whether because of my anger at seeing a former comrade in an enemy uniform or just my embarrassing situation before this company, with whom we had in Cuxhaven not been very good neighbours, when they pulled up and asked in a quite friendly manner if I was hurt and offered to help me find my horse, I rose abruptly from my ditch and said that my sole wish was to be left alone. On that they laughed and, saluting, rode on.

The corvette sailed the next morning, and shortly thereafter our two gunboats also continued their voyage. Because of a false report that numerous Italian vessels were moving in the same direction through the Ionian Sea, we sped along, hugging the Albanian coast. Many times smoke was seen on the horizon, and then *Reka* and *Dalmat* would move closer to the land. All the crew would be on deck, the officers on the bridge, and whoever disposed of a glass would anxiously search the outlines of the sinister wanderer, out there on the high seas. Only in Lissa[12] did we learn that war had not yet come and possibly might not come at all. Nonetheless, we believed it would, and always happens in such cases, it was better to follow our wishes than some other man's assertions. This wish was named: War and Tegetthoff.

---

11 *Korvetten-Kapitän* in Austrian German. The rank was introduced by the decree of 21 March 1866.
12 Vis, Croatia.

When the gunboats came in sight of the Istrian coast, the green velvet hills climbing out of the sea, every heart beat faster. We passed the southern point of the peninsula and the rocky island of Porer. Then, as we neared the entrance, an imperial ironclad rounded Cape Compare.[13] Her deep black hull and black smoke seemed to the optimistic to be the first longed-for stormcloud. Then a wooden frigate sailed from the roads of Fasana,[14] and now you could see other ships lying at anchor there. Pola was in an uproar![15]

---

13 Rt. Kumpar, Croatia, the entrance to Pula harbour. A mole now extends north to partially close off the entrance.
14 Fažanski Kanal, Croatia.
15 The order for the imperial fleet to be armed and prepared had gone out on 30 April 1866, quite late in Austrian preparations for war, as Rottauscher later remarks.

9

The navy arms against Italy

As *Dalmat* and *Reka* ran into Pola, there stretched before them a scene of the busiest activity. Steaming slowly through the tumult, we were all filled with impressions: here vessels being rigged, there peniches[1] full of coal, fresh water and ammunition, towed by rowing boats, there again cranes groaning. The hot summer day reposed with meditative calm. Only one thing attracted our curiosity – who would be squadron commander? Because Tegetthoff was too junior in rank and years, there was little hope he would be chosen.

According to an old custom, the gunboats dropped anchor opposite the arsenal and the captains went onshore to present their reports. Those left behind crowded the deck: the same fever gripped officers and men. People talked, smoking and looking at the unusual activity in the harbour, their only wish to lay hold of some news. Finally a boat passed within shouting distance, and the midshipman in it waved both hands in greeting.

"What news?" we shouted across.

"Everything's to be fitted out!" came over the water, "Tegetthoff's squadron commander!"

For a second we were speechless with joy, but then we shouted in triumph – we were under our lucky star, and people shouted the beloved name to those behind them and shook hands, extremely happy. The captain returned and confirmed the glad tidings. There were promotions daily. When I went ashore that afternoon, I always found friends who had been midshipmen when I had left but who were now officers. The booths of the red Jew Fanganel looked like a Christmas market, for they contained only gold swordknots, epaulettes, sabres and sashes. There was unbelievable movement buzzing through the lanes – the forts' ammunition carts trundled by, orderlies ran, and wooden barracks had been erected before the town for the reservists. These men, still in their Dalmatian costume or gondoliers' smocks, were at every corner, greeting the officers with a certain familiar comradeliness and besieging the wine shops. A friend took me under the arm and we ran to the Gaudenz, I burning for news and he as thirsty to get the best the café had to offer. In the same room on which we had lived on bread and coffee during our most wretched period, we were given ices, and then a bottle of rosé wine.

He told me how gloomy things had been when the first rumours of war had flared up. While the land forces were arming, nothing was happening with the navy. Every phase brought the feeling: flickering hopes and the fear they would not be ready for action, not be allowed to gain the ascendancy over the Italians as the result of a prohibition of being allowed to take the offensive. In fact, indeed, at the start of June there were but five ironclads to oppose 12 enemy ones.

At last, Archduke Leopold[2] had resigned command of the navy and took over a corps. It was said he had not occupied himself at all with the fleet, but such was not the case,

---

1 An oared boat capable of sea travel with a schooner rig.
2 Archduke Leopold of Austria (1823–98), a cousin of the emperor, was made commander of the navy in 1865. As Rottauscher remarks, the archduke was first and foremost a military man (he was head of

rather the reverse. The prince was in a council of senior officers chaired by His Majesty, where he told it that anything could be expected of the navy if it was given Tegetthoff as commander. I must, however, emphasize that this was a later rumour which cannot be confirmed. But stop – suffice it to say that people still believe it. Archduke Leopold had not thought the navy was to be taken seriously because of the war over the tunic. The history of this piece of clothing is as follows. Anything that reminded one of the army was deemed unnaval; the navy stressed its differences from the army. The sailors gave the soldiers the sarcastic name of *pagnocca* (army bread), and most of we officers would have nothing at all to do with them. To declare externally we were sea-dogs and hence above all a form of dilettante, we walked hands in pockets, dragging our sabres and waving our caps to each other in greeting. Whoever was quickest to cause insurmountable confusion in a landed company was admired by his brother officers. When we marched in review, a horde would trudge by those reviewing us. But now Archduke Leopold had come – he was used to army ways, and at first he was horrified, then enraged. In order to break the navy of its habit of civilian allure, it was ordered that a high-collared infantry tunic was to be worn. We were deeply mortified; there were secret meetings and minor conspiracies. It was held naval traditions were being attacked, and other things, and some of us thought quite seriously of resigning. At the head of the uprising was a lieutenant who had been given the honourable name of the fleet's shark. Now this fleet's shark, as if to advertise his personality, always appeared in a frock coat so long that he flitted through Pola like a bat, stirring everyone to resistance. Moreover, we had been allowed to wear out the old clothing, and so the tunic was little worn and died from this passive resistance. It was known that Archduke Leopold resented this opposition. Now, very soon before the war, he had been transferred to the army. We had had no expectation of any intercession, and it was said the navy was condemned to inactivity and a defensive posture almost as a punishment.

Suddenly, however, Tegetthoff was summoned to Vienna and returned as commander in chief of the fleet. Depression vanished in the boundless joy with which he was greeted. A storm of high spirits rushed through Pola; the ships tore themselves free from the land, the funnels smoked, people ran about the decks like industrious ants, and countless coal carriers and steamers filled with workmen came over from the Venice arsenal. Repairs were quickly made, telegrams whipped on the construction of *Erzherzog Max* and *Habsburg*, which were still in the Triest shipyard. As soon as a vessel was ready, it sailed for Fasana, dropped anchor and began to fire live rounds. Tegetthoff, Eberan,[3] the commandant of the arsenal, and the port admiral, Baron Bourgignon, were, my comrade told me, seemingly everywhere at the same time; there was not an hour's rest. And this was necessary, for once more there was a profound lack of money and material. Hammocks had to be hung around the main bridges as protection from splinters, and the wooden ships were armoured with chains. I was flabbergasted by this latter measure – it reminded me of the legendary

---

the engineer corps) and so was not that sympathetic to the outlook of the naval officer corps. However, he did work on plans for the fleet's employment in the 1866 war. Contrary to Rottauscher's assertion, Leopold did not resign until 1868, when he was replaced by Tegetthoff.

3   Alexander Eberan von Eberhorst (1829–1914), an Austrian naval officer since 1847, had been promoted commander in 1860, and in June (later July) 1866 a captain. As Rottauscher remarks, he was hugely involved in preparing the fleet for war with Italy, as director of fitting out vessels at Pola since August 1865. Eberan was promoted admiral in 1896 and retired the following year after a very distinguished career. He received very much praise from Tegetthoff and other officers for his speedy fitting-out of the fleet, and so perhaps may be seen as another of the architects of the victory at Lissa.

efforts of classical navies. And yet the thing was true, as I soon saw with my own eyes. The sides of the frigates seemed as wrinkled as the skins of old dinosaurs....

Chain after chain was bound tightly betweeen the gunports with long nails. While in the roads firing at targets was taking place to starboard, to port the workmen were hanging on and driving in the halters to the sound of gunfire. One ship, the *Novara*, even fought at Lissa with railway ties bolted to her sides. The reason why such a singular clothing was adopted was told to me right after the other person had learned why, and indeed in such an excited way and in such detail that only official sources could persuade me, I had not been there at the time. And yet I did experience it! Or was it that it was within the bounds of my memory, and what was reported was quite thrown into confusion?

During this period, *Novara* was on the bank being fitted out. A number of officers, myself included, were sitting at our midday meal in an inn – at least I remember it as such. Suddenly there was a blaring of horns and a ringing of bells; officers and midshipmen ran out of all the inns and taverns, men streamed from the ships, the chains of the wooden frigates were left hanging, boats shot over to drag away the imperilled one – *Novara* was burning! The glowing red ship was grappled on all sides while being splashed with water by people on the other vessels. But the blaze could not be mastered, and large launches came up to sink the *Novara* with gunfire. They lay very close and fired continuously at the frigate's waterline, and then the vessel was repeatedly grappled. I do not know how the fire was put out, despite the flames and the rain of burning wooden shavings – suffice it to say that it was, with the energy of despair. But *Novara* had been gutted, and the Austrian fleet had one less warship. But I recollect exactly that no one complained or was troubled, so great was Tegetthoff's influence.

The following day the wreck was towed to Triest. The officer commanding her brought an order that she was to be handed over in six weeks in battleworthy condition. The Tonello yard[4] punctually carried out this enormous task, and soon after the start of the war the *Novara* returned to the squadron, armoured with railway ties for lack of any better material.

I remember all of this precisely; it lives in me almost as if I had been there. But I cannot reconcile the date with the calendar, for according to one official source, *Novara* must have burned three days before my arrival.[5]

There was no doubt, and it was certainly correct, about who had set the fire. The blame was laid on the workmen of the arsenal at Venice, who had always been turbulent and who in 1848 had killed their commandant.[6] Their revolutionary spirit was so astonishing when you compared them to the other Venetians in the navy and army, that they could at the same time be on good terms with their colleagues. They composed gracious comic poems about our risky undertaking, had relatives on the vessels; they spared nothing to throw obstacles in our way. Some of the noblemen, who were perhaps still in mourning for the republic, made no distinction between the navy and the army.

---

4 The Trieste shipyard founded by Giuseppe Tonello (died 1870), was from 1840 named the San Marco yard, and was then incorporated as the Cantiere Navale Adriatico. It was extremely important to the navy and built every one of the seven Austrian ironclads which fought at Lissa, but then declined after the owner's death and was sold in 1875.

5 Official accounts state that *Novara* was sabotaged on 3 May 1866.

6 Captain Johann Ritter von Marinovich (born 1792) had indeed been killed by the workmen of the arsenal in 1848, when Venice rose in revolt against its Austrian overlords. But to be fair, it should be remarked that Marinovich was an extremely harsh and tactless man who had made himself hated by the workers.

But on this, although I am speaking once more about it, I must say also that the aversion to the infantry never found expression in acts of murder such as it did in the rest of Italy. The Venetians are a kind-hearted, cheerful people, and their marked sense of humour helps them get over many things. For instance, once some Croats organized a pillaging expedition by having one of them enter the Riva degli Schiavoni in full uniform. It had just stopped raining, and there were puddles among the stones. The honest man calmly paid out a line, baited it and tossed the hook into a puddle – and this among a population of fishermen! Everyone ran over, shouted and yelled, "Fish, Croat, fish!" The entire area was black with men who streamed there and doubled up with laughter. And yet on the Croat fished.

Suddenly a shrill whistle sounded, the peerless sportsman reeled in his line with dignity and, smiling, went away, followed by the frenzied crowd. But when the latter left him and returned to their stalls, moaning and weeping broke out along the entire line: the rascal's comrades had cleaned out their premises in the meantime. You would have thought that the indignation would have lasted, but not a bit of it! "Fish, Croat" became a stock phrase, and people always laughed at it.

But now I turn again to the tumult of the fitting out. Despite the conspiracy on the *Novara*, the Venetian sailors and workmen remained, the former because they were in no way to blame for it and the latter because there was neither time nor money to replace them. We had to be content with supervising them closely.

The day after the one on which I spent pleasant hours chatting in the old café, I was transferred to the wooden frigate *Adria* as a midshipman who was performing the duties of an officer. She was already in the roads, and for the first time I was received at the entry port with due ceremony. I stepped on board past the two sailors and the saluting petty officer as if I was now a great lord. Shortly thereafter I was made a sub lieutenant.

Tegetthoff had hoisted his flag on the *Schwarzenberg*. Now all day long on board her there were examinations of anyone who had not proved his capability as I had. One hundred and twenty midshipmen were handed officers' commissions in the wink of an eye in Fasana; only one did not pass. He had answered every question with the solemn, calm answer of "I do not know" and so was thrown out.[7]

And the fleet assembled and grew stronger, the vessels recently built and rebuilt joining the squadron. The ironclads *Habsburg* and *Ferdinand Max* and the wooden battleship *Kaiser* were greeted in a brilliant festival, each one of them rousing our hopes almost to ecstasy. Admittedly they were only half ready, admittedly they lacked interior fittings, admittedly some of the armour was so poor that a speculator must have done it with extreme deliberation. But what did that matter? Of all their faults, only one now filled us with wrath and an angry hatred of Prussia, whose government had prohibited the delivery of guns from Krupp. Instead of the 100-pounders which nearly all the Italian ironclads had, the ships were armed with smoothbore 48-pounders. But once again, what did that matter? When *Ferdinand Max* arrived, Tegetthoff had hoisted his flag in her, and since then she had been completed.

A heavy summer storm passed over the squadron, rain lashing the dripping planks of the deck and the watch. From hanging cloud banks bursting away sharply, our shots flashed from the gunports, and the balls skipped twice, three times with fountains of spray over the dark sea. All day long the echoes of gunfire boomed through the marshy woods

---

7   In March 1866, according to official states, there were 202 midshipmen on the navy's rolls.

of the Brioni Islands.[8] Mines were laid in front of Pola, and two ships were constantly on duty as pickets, one to the north, the other to the south, and the fleet kept banked fires in all of its boilers. We may still have been at peace, but no one trusted the enemy. An enterprising chap had set up a beerhall in Fasana, and in its garden we played Boccia, Italian bowls, sat around and drank.

In the main square, the horses of the Seressaners,[9] who belonged to the fortress command, were tied up. These wild fellows lounged about in the sun and dust, wearing their vermilion cloaks and with household knives and silver-mounted pistols stuck into their belts.

And the wind brought from Pola the tumult of an alarm. The sky became red; this time someone had set fire to the arsenal. The next day, from on board we saw the Seressaners gliding through the brushwood like spots of blood, searching. Many also rode into the shallows, to poke with their Handjars[10] into the overhanging bushes. I do not know if the perpetrator was caught. But it was as if it was in the time of a primeval, long-vanished beauty, the men and horses rolling in from the deeper blue like foam, the horses wet to above their chests and the men's red cloaks fluttering.

We knew next to nothing of the enemy, or only that which had been reported in foreign journals. Nothing about where their fleet lay, nothing about the degree of preparations for war in Ancona, which we assumed the Italians had chosen as their main harbour. Rumours circulated about the colossal measurements of the latest Italian ironclad, *Re d'Italia*,[11] and about her frightful armament of thirty 100-pounders. The papers reported no less dreadful news about the ram *Affondatore*,[12] whose ram, it was said, could sink every wooden ship in the world.

Then one evening all the lighthouses along the coast were extinguished at a blow. If before you had often seen their beams playing over the sea when you were on the night watch, now all slept in deepest darkness, and it was as dead and desolate as if you were on a faraway, uncharted sea, the shoals menacing any vessel which passed by outside the roads. Only the signal lights flashed and danced around the squadron from poop deck to poop deck. When nature abandons itself to breathe deeper, now there called the thousand shrill voices of the night from the nearby brushwood, while the sea washed dully over the shore. And through it all, the clanging of the bells of the watches from deck to deck.

From 11 June, although war had not been formally declared, a state of war existed with Prussia. Every day we hoped to read about actions.

---

8   Brijuni, Croatia, now a national park and popular tourist destination.

9   A branch of the frontier infantry, the *Serežaners*, to give their proper name, were their elite who were employed as scouts and policemen.

10 A long, wide-bladed knife common to the western Balkans. The word is *handžar* in Serbo-Croat.

11 Completed in 1864 in an American yard, *Re d'Italia* and her sister ship *Re di Portogallo* were in 1866 the Italian navy's most powerful units. They were approximately 5 600 tonnes, with 38 cannon and a crew of 550.

12 This vessel had originally been designed as an unarmoured ram but had received two massive turrets during the course of her reconstruction. Launched in 1866 and barely in time for Lissa, the *Affondatore* was an extremely powerful vessel which was unfortunately mishandled during the battle and so had little effect. She was 4 070 tonnes, with two 25.4 cm (10 in) cannon and a crew of 356. The *Affondatore* sank at her moorings in August 1866, and was then twice rebuilt before being stricken in 1907 as a torpedo tender.

My brother was a cuirassier in the North Army.[13] Perhaps Venice's future had already been contended for in Bohemia. I repeat: Venice's future. For what did the house of cards of the Germanic Confederation and the supremacy in Germany mean to us, for which, incidentally, the war seemed to have been fought? We did not foresee anything else than that the fate of the south would be decided in the south.

Many times when there was no moon at night, it was magically light. How with a soft blue oversnowed then lay the sea and the rocks. An amazing veil, woven as if it had been for a fable, was wafted from things, making them bodiless and dreamlike. Then as the guards moved here and there they became wandering, shadowless figures, only their rifle barrels shimmering. Singing cicadas, lured from their perches in the trees by the magical light, fell pattering onto the deck planks.

At last, on 23 June, the captain stood on an upturned water cask, we officers beside him, sashes around our hips. There was a wider circle of barefooted sailors, all of whom had run up and were pressing around. Some of them climbed over the man in front, and some were even hanging from the rigging in order to hear. In such a way was the start of hostilities with Italy made known.

For the last time, now under German officers, did this fleet, for centuries mistress of the Levant, and with its same sailors as in days gone past, Venetians and Slavs, throw itself at the enemy. And its admiral was no lesser man that all its commanders, who had stormed Constantinople and conquered Cyprus and the archipelagoes.[14] His stiffly pointing finger was a hypnotizing command, and we would follow him without hesitation into any danger, into fire and gunsmoke.

---

13 Ferdinand Rottauscher (born 1844) was educated at the Wiener Neustadt military academy near Vienna and in 1864 departed to become a junior lieutenant in the 11th Cuirassier Regiment of the Austrian army. As such, he displayed notable bravery at the battles of Nachod and Königgrätz during the 1866 campaign.

14 A rather overdone attempt to imply that the Austrian fleet in 1866 was the successor to the great Venetian fleets of the Middle Ages and Renaissance.

10

The Italian attack on Lissa

Suddenly the rumour fluttered about that Italian ships were attacking Lissa and that the news had been confirmed by official despatches. Everyone drew a deep breath, for now we said we knew to a certainty that the very next telegram would announce the blockade of Triest. The enemy's intention seemed quite clear; they wanted to decoy us away from Dalmatia by false reports so as to be able to attack the Southern Railway[1] without hindrance. Thus we thought, and we waited excitedly for the moment when the fleet would be summoned north. Boat after boat sped here and there between the flagship and Brioni, and the telegraph operators of the forts were constantly working. And always there came this strange report: Italian ships are bombarding Lissa. This was no trick; it came from the island's garrison, the entire enemy squadron was pounding the isle's feeble works.

Telegrams flew to and from all corners of the earth, Vienna, headquarters of South Army, Lissa. But at 2 P.M. on 18 July the despatches from Dalmatia ceased. Right in the middle of a telegram, the machine halted, as if the skeletal hand of Death had silenced it and its chatter of words had dried up. The submarine cable had been cut.

We kept up our buzz of questions if Triest or Lissa was the fleet's destination, if we were not speculating too much and would cold-bloodedly let the island's weak garrison perish as a result.

Three hours later the Dalmatian telegraph began to work again, and the boats hastened more quickly. We were always on deck, and the noise of the men rose from the gunports like a captive swarm of bees. The deep fever of blood and battles had hold of us, and every moment was a delirious frenzy. At short intervals, there rushed from the sea the rumbling sounds of those ships which the day before had been firing at anchored targets. It was learned that in fact the Italians had destroyed the cable between Lissa and the closest island, Lesina,[2] and one of their ships had even run into Lesina in order to there also destroy the communication with Tegetthoff. But this second attempt the enemy had not executed correctly, and moreover with unnecessary elaboration. Instead of falling on the post office at night, they appeared in broad daylight, first threatening a bombardment and then formally disembarking troops. The official slipped away with the machines and fled to a good look-out point, continuing to send despatches about what he could descry of events at Lissa. Peasants and policemen lay around him in the rocks, rifles at the ready, but this precaution was unnecessary, for the Italians had already embarked, satisfied that the postal official and his telegraph were not there. They did not bother with the cable linking Lesina to the mainland. Now quickly one after the other the official reported that an Austrian battery had blown up, that the enemy was still shelling the harbour and that he had counted 22 vessels. To speak plainly, we were stunned by this unheard-of,

---

1   Completed in 1857, this railway linked Vienna and Trieste and during the war was extremely important for bringing men, horses and supplies to the southern theatre.
2   Hvar, Croatia.

quite unbelievable news. The enemy squadron was investing a rocky eyrie and was hotly pursuing a fruitless operation. We sat up all night in the wardroom, discussing the matter we had been forced to believe and yet did not want to with all manner of intensity.

The following morning I was ordered on board the battleship *Kaiser*, which commanded we wooden frigates. I was to make corrections to the secret signal books and similar items, and every ship had been required to send an officer for that purpose. When I climbed on board, midshipmen from the entire wooden division were standing about, to whom the less important circular orders had been handed previously. Each had his map under his arm, and they obviously did not want to leave the source of the news which was awaited so eagerly and were whispering to one another. I passed through them and went down to the wardroom. There the company had just dipped their pens in ink and had gone to the right place on the page, and the supervisor had just ended the first line of his dictation, when the door was pushed open and the wide rays of a blinding sun streamed into the room. On the step stood Sub Lieutenant Proch, hanging onto the doorjamb with both hands. He yelled down, "Raise steam and load with shot – we're going out!" He was one of the first to fall in the battle; hit between his eyes by a bullet, he crashed from the mizzen mast to the after deck like a lump of lead and lay there with a shattered skull. It was as if a shell had exploded among us – we leaped up, banged back our chairs and knocked over an inkpot, so that its black stream ran over the table and dripped onto the oaken planks. Everyone grabbed their caps and fell over one another to get to the entry port. There all the rowing boats were crashing and squeezing against one another – each crew wanted to get away with their officer before the others. From the funnels the first trails of smoke were already beginning to rise; engines were working, everywhere around there was movement, a running here and there around the decks, while my boat shot between the tall sides as if through a maze. The last signal had just disappeared from *Ferdinand Max*'s mast, and many times the sun was visible only in the ever denser whirl of smoke as if through a browned glass.

The flagship remained in the roads so as to receive or send last-minute despatches with Brioni, but as soon as every other vessel was clear she raised anchor. A loud rattling ran through the squadron; the first ships were already making for the exit from the roads. A short time later the vessels had assembled in the open sea south of Brioni and were steaming quite slowly towards the Istrian coast, waiting patiently for Tegetthoff.

Exactly at 1 the admiral appeared behind us. Bursting forth from the foam of gorse of the islands of the reefs, the *Ferdinand Max* shoved the water aside with her bow. As at the last review, Tegetthoff stood on the rear casemate of his ironclad, his confidants grouped around him. We recognized every one of them through a glass: Sterneck, Lindner,[3]

---

3   Karl Lindner (1831–98). Lindner became a naval officer in 1857, and in 1862 commanding officer of the *Seehund*. A commander from 1864, he took part in the Schleswig-Holstein war and was ennobled for his services, and then in 1866 he was adjutant to Tegetthoff. Lindner retired in 1869 but was back the next year and became captain of the *Habsburg*. He was made a vice admiral in 1883.

Attelmayer,[4] Spaun,[5] Minitullo.[6] The signal midshipmen, Görz[7] and Sinkowsky,[8] stood to one side rummaging through the pile of flags. Thus *Ferdinand Max* came pounding along, black as night, through the squadron from its tail to its head. Just now the colossus seems to me somewhat at variance with the grey used in modern times. Then all at once, without any order, all hatchways opened and a trampling mob rushed from the depths of the ships – the men ran onto the deck and stormed ever higher into the rigging; ever more there crawled hundreds and hundreds. They seemed to had lost their senses, and the stretching of their hands and the jubilation rose ever higher. On the ships which had bands, their members rushed together and played the national anthem. Tegetthoff took off his cap and waved it in wide circles. Sweeping by like a storm, inundated with jubilation, exposed to the utter discord of the confused music, the flagship rushed to the head of the squadron.

But once she had reached there the noise stopped as if cut off by a knife, and the bands ceased in mid-note, and the masses of men rippled back to the decks. Then there was breathless silence. One after the other, the signals quickly flew to order the formation of the three concentric chevrons in which the squadron would steam. In the first chevron the ironclads, *Ferdinand Max* at their head; in the second we frigates, leg by *Kaiser*; and in the third the seven gunboats, taken all together a wooden roundshot covered in iron. Within a few moments, and precisely and exactly, there followed the necessary movements, and then the fleet went to full speed.

But there was then an extremely amusing incident, for suddenly there limped out of the entrance to Pola harbour, her engine rumbling, the steamer *Vulkan*.[9] She was an ancient blockade-runner now used only as a bulk transport between Fasana and the arsenal, no longer allowed to take to the open sea and armed with two small guns from a day long since past. These guns flashed, brilliantly polished, as *Vulkan* strenuously came up, panting as heavily as if each turn of the screw would be her last rattling breath. We thought she was bringing an important despatch and was therefore expending all her feeble strength to groan after us. But instead she hoisted the timid question whether she might be allowed to join the squadron. We broke into shouts of laughter. *Ferdinand Max* answered shortly, "No," which stopped her dead in her tracks, shocked by such a boorish reply. As we ploughed south at full speed, leaving behind us a gigantic white wake and enveloped in a sea of smoke, the clouds of the first shower rising on the horizon and

---

4   Ferdinand Attlmayer (Attlmayr) (1829–1906), then a lieutenant, went on to a career as an author, and one of his works was about the Adriatic naval campaign of 1866.

5   Hermann Freiherr von Spaun (1833–1919) entered the navy in 1850, and in 1860 was promoted lieutenant. He was second in command of the *Ferdinand Max* at Lissa and was slightly wounded. Spaun went on to a notable career in the navy, serving as naval minister between 1897 and 1904 and doing much to lay the foundations for the Austro-Hungarian fleet which fought in World War I. He was promoted admiral in 1899.

6   Franz Freiherr von Minutillo (1840–1916) joined the navy in 1857, and in June 1866 he was promoted lieutenant first class. At Lissa he served as Tegetthoff's personal adjutant and was badly wounded in the right wrist when the *Ferdinand Max* rammed the *Re d'Italia*. Promoted admiral in 1904, he retired the next year.

7   Konstantin Ritter von Görz, decorated for the 1864 and 1866 campaigns and a commander by 1890.

8   Midshipman Karl von Sinkovsky.

9   This vessel had been chartered from the Austrian Lloyd at the start of the war and was returned to that company after it.

blowing around us, we saw the *Vulkan* gazing sadly after us, lying in the sun beneath the shining yellow crags.

11

Before the battle

A fresh contrary wind and sea became ever more noticeable, making it harder for the wooden frigates, not just to maintain the prescribed speed of eight knots, but also to keep the distance between the ships, which was only two cables.[1] Showers passed over us even more rapidly, and afternoon blended into night under dirty colours. Only deep in the west was there a lighter band above the horizon, and this followed us, even though in the meantime it became quite dark. In the evening the bugle sounded for roll call, and the men went to their action stations. The officers paced here and there, checking the rifles and the gun equipment for the last time. On the half deck (the third deck from the top) there lay ready wooden plugs such as were used to stop leaks and which played an important role in naval battles of that era. Men spoke in low tones, but often they were drowned out by a loud shout.

At last the waiting men were told they could rest but not undress; everyone had to be at his post. The possibility that we could meet the enemy, here at the halfway point at Porto Tajer,[2] was not excluded. There were reasons for such a consideration: Lissa might have fallen, or the bombardment might have been broken off. In fact, the possibility of a night action was still nearer! The Lesina harbour officials, who had been interrogated by the landing detachment, had stated that Tegetthoff had promised he would come to their relief. I do not know why, therefore, the Italians nonetheless remained before Lissa.

I walked to and fro along the deck with a brother officer for some time, the wooden planks reflecting every wet imprint of our soles. Under the first casemate, there were crouching some Ruthenian[3] naval infantrymen turning a grindstone and once more sharpening their unwieldy *Haubajonette*,[4] in one of which one of them was reflected. Then we descended into the wardroom and ate, not speaking much. Finally, wine was handed around, the lanterns swaying monotonously back and forth as the cabin rose and fell. From time to time we heard the clanging of the engine commands, and so we sat around the table, one of us leaning his forehead on his outstretched arm and another tipped back in his chair, and talked about the chances of the coming day.

Then the bosun came in bearing stoppers and woollen blankets against leaks and fire. One of us asked him what he thought would have happened by that time the next day. His right cheek full of tobacco, the old seaman shrugged and growled, "The Italians will have been beaten," as if it were the most absurd question in the world. Someone commented it would be smarter for us officers not to undress either. Then we broke up, and the servant removed the plates and glasses and for a long time washed them in the

---

1   366 m; 400 yds.
2   Luka Telascika, Croatia.
3   A contemporary term for what are now western Ukrainians, or Rusyns.
4   An untranslatable term for the short, wide bayonet carried by some branches of the Austrian military. The bayonet was shorter and wider than those of the infantry because its rifle was shorter than that of the infantry, and so the increased length and width allowed the bayonet to be used in the same way as the one of the infantry rifle.

adjoining pantry. I went topside alone to see what the men were doing. On the darkest step stood the supervisory midshipman, his greatcoat loose about his shoulders and in this lonely spot seemingly absorbed in thoughts of something pleasant, for he took not the slightest notice of me as I passed by to the rumble of the engine. Melancholy songs crowded in on me in a low chorus – the Dalmatians were singing. It was their ancient heroic song of Kraljevic Marko,[5] of victories over the Turks and battles against pashas in the Karst. Every uniform song they therefore hummed, strewn in groups around every gun, while the stifling night air oppressed one and the deck rocked. Crouched apart from them were the few Venetians of the gun deck. They neither spoke nor sang, only from time to time whispering among themselves about something, as children will sit together and whisper ghost stories.

On entering my cabin, I threw myself fully clothed on the bed, but sleep shunned me. It was if the engine was pounding more heavily, as if the odour of the still wet paint of our chain armour was stronger. When at last I did fall into a confused half-doze, my servant banged on the door. My watch said 11:45, and I had the dog watch,[6] so up I jumped. When I left, I found the midshipman of the watch ready. The servant had brewed the customary black coffee, and we drank it leisurely. Then midnight struck, clear and ringing. When we climbed the companionway, a rainbow greeted us for a second. I relieved my very tired predecessor, who had been ruling over the miserable night, and began my stroll.

On the poop of every vessel, lanterns were burning, as had been ordered, and we had to steer after them in a darkness in which you could not see your hand in front of your face, taking them as the right way to maintain formation. The engine-room telegraph clanged continuously; at one time the frigate would speed up, at another it would slow. There was nothing other than the thick, heavy dark, in which the after lanterns swam as if the three chevrons were bound to the sea by burning nails.

Nothing was so omnipresent as the roaring of the waves stirred up around us and invisible from afar, and the air was not as damp, seeming to be impregnated with the coal dust of the smoke which fell all around. The fact that we were continuously covered in a dense mist could only be noticed by the smell and by the glutinous brown paste which evermore increased the dull shine of the glowing disk of the bridge compass. In short, you saw neither the outline of the ironclad running before you nor the silhouettes of the islands, which we often passed by very close. A new shower always pattered over the deck. You heard it drumming ahead of you, felt its drops beating quickly in your face and heard it pass away behind you, leaving silence once more in its wake. Nothing but the call of the watch wailed over the squadron, nothing but ships' bells rang the half hours. Then suddenly the light tone of the bronze bell used from 2100 for 12 hours began to be heard.

Below the bridge the helmsman, whispering with his men, turned the wheel with a creak; from time to time there sang in the rigging a cicada, still sitting on the mast from the bushy woods of Brioni.

---

5   Marko Kraljević (died 1395), king of Serbia from 1371 to 1395 and a national hero who was a fierce foe of the Turkish invaders. His exploits have made him legendary in the literature and traditions of the southern Slavs, and many folk songs, ballads and poems have been written about him.

6   Austrian practice differed from that of the Royal Navy, which counted two dog watches, from 4 to 6 and from 6 to 8 P.M. The watch which Rottauscher was starting was called the middle watch in British naval practice.

Since we had come about halfway and were now on a level with Porto Tajer, we imagined that any second we would hear the first gunshot, to any second see from ahead the signal winking for action. But the flashing lights were concerned with other orders.

At last the pitch-black night began to lighten, and the first frost of morning was expelled in deep breaths across the bridge. Like hazy shadow figures, the ever-more distant ships glided along, and now for the first time you saw the nearest of them, plunging through the wave-grazing clouds, and then others emerged, while the nearest regained its dark colour and you could see men moving about on its deck. A piece of mother-of-pearl sky became visible through the rushing clouds for some seconds.

The bells rang once more: eight bells, 4 A.M. Our relief came, and as the men climbed up the swaying ladders the wind tore hard at their greatcoats. I could not give my relief, Midshipman Count Montecuccoli,[7] any information, for the last log entry had showed only five and a half nautical miles[8] from Fasana, and since then we had steamed 85 nautical miles.[9] Plus the sea was contrary; already larger foam-topped crests were dancing about.

I went to my cabin and had a wash, for my face and hands had been blackened by the smoke rolling over the deck and sea. Then, weary and freezing, I wrapped myself in my greatcoat, threw myself on my bed and sank into a deathlike sleep. Towards 9 I heard Montecuccoli's voice. When I asked what the weather was like, he said still rain, rain and a swelling sea. But all the same, we could fall on the Italians in an hour. A Lloyd steamer coming from Lissa had been stopped by the scout *Stadion*.[10] It had confirmed the enemy was still before Lissa, so we held our course.

I went promptly to the door and called the servant. Then we sat down in the wardroom and ate as much as we could, for once the enemy was sighted and the powder magazines were opened there would be no more hot food.

The Lloyd steamer of which Montecuccoli had spoken had the previous night been fired on in error by the fortifications of Lissa. Right afterwards she had sighted the Italian squadron and had counted its vessels, but without being annoyed by it. A funny story was later told about this incident. The next day the captain of this ship was sitting in a coffeehouse in Triest. "I had," he called out, "seen the enemy, and then our own ships. Then I crossed myself and said to my mate, 'The poor Austrian fleet!'" But just as he was saying this, the street urchins were yelling about the victory at Lissa and selling special editions. This man had given us the best testimony, we with our chains and railway ties driving towards a most modern fleet.

The two of us were still in the wardroom when all at once some men ran by and we heard the alarm on all sides. We rushed outside – "The Italians are in sight!" someone yelled. We ran through the gundeck, where stood ready small, low tubs of watered wine and biscuit, with which the men could refresh themselves in action. "Where are the Italians?" we shouted to a midshipman as we leaped onto the deck. He said they were still not in sight; only a scout had given the signal.

---

7   Rudolf Count Montecuccoli degli Erri (1843–1922). Entering the navy in 1857, Montecuccoli embarked on a career which would lead him to the highest rank. Rottauscher is incorrect to call him a midshipman, since he too had been promoted sub lieutenant in March 1866. Montecuccoli was awarded a medal for his bravery at Lissa, and he rose to become a full admiral in 1905 and naval minister between 1904 and 1913, so having an extremely important influence on the imperial navy which fought in World War I.

8   10.2 km; 6.3 miles.

9   158 km; 97.3 miles.

10 Chartered from the Lloyd in 1859 and 1866 as a scout, this vessel was 1 400 tonnes and was unarmed.

Everyone crowded to the rail. The scout was seen far ahead in the smoke, and we saw through glasses how signals were going up and down her masts all the time. She had very much shortened course and seemed as she wanted to creep into the squadron's mass. The contrary wind blew perceptibly. In the distance you could see at Lissa the edge of the front, a point in the Adriatic at which the air currents frequently change. A stoical sailor sat in a boat, got rid of the rainwater and then cleaned it as calmly as if he had all day.

At that moment a shout of people sucking in their breath ran through the frigate. As if the curtain of a theatre had parted, suddenly there opened from heaven to sea a gigantic fissure of the deepest blue. Dazzled, we saw in the distance the line of the Italian ironclads steaming off Lissa, looking like tiny light grey tin toys, running in a long line one after the other. But before we could count them, before the enemy's wooden ships could be made out, before the island's bare mountains were implanted on our eyes, the ray was covered by a cloud, which coming from behind rushed over us and enveloped us in darkness. The wind had veered round; a rainbow arched over us from the after deck to the fore deck. Covered by it, in blowing wind and water, the squadron hastened towards the enemy. Ever more the showers pattered down on the sterns of the ships; the engines worked hastily, their powerful rattling in tone. Before us the smoke was dispersing over the leading ships, which were pitching heavily all the time. Now the rainbow overtook the fleet, pushing before us like a black screen towards Lissa, the imperial squadron leaving the brightly shining sun. In this screen, the flagship, driving its bow into the clouds, was just like a black silhouette. She signalled "Clear ship for action!" and all answered "Clear ship for action!" Then she signalled the ironclads "Armoured ships will ram the enemy and sink them!", and they replied "Armoured ships will ram the enemy and sink them!"

Alarm bugles blared. We heard one, then another, and then many, sound ever louder the more the signals from *Ferdinand Max* were echoed through the fleet, and finally all the ships caught hold of the notes.

The gunports flew open, and on the spray-drenched, sun-dappled sky there arose on every mast bales of cloth, which whipped out in the usurping wind to dress overall every ship. All was a light, colourful stream of flags blowing from back to front. Once more *Ferdinand Max* showed a signal, the word "Must" – it was to begin the announcement "There must be a victory at Lissa." But at the same time the rainbow stumbled away to starboard, to the open sea. Lissa and the enemy fleet lay before us; the flagship's signalman had no time left to complete the sentence. For some seconds the brazen word "must" swished at the point of the wedge, simultaneously showing us where Tegetthoff was, but then it was pulled down, and nothing else followed.

The officers shook hands with each other, and then everyone hastened to his post. But before I went below deck, I cast a last glance at the enemy. Close inshore to Lissa there moved in total confusion around one point the Italian wooden vessels. They were surrounding a large transport steamer, the *Piemonte*, which as we later learned had been running beside our fleet for part of the night and which was carrying 500 naval infantrymen who were to storm the fortifications.

Around this steamer, therefore, there flocked the Italian wooden ships, speedily pulling in the landing forces to themselves, and so deprived of fighting efficiency that for the entire battle they remained to one side and abandoned the ironclads to their fate.[11]

---

11 Rottauscher's is one explanation for the inactivity of the Italian wooden squadron. It has also been suggested that the commander of the squadron, Vice Admiral Giovanni Battista Count Albini (1812–76),

For their part, the latter were still steaming in line ahead, just like we had seen them before. Now they too dressed overall, but in such a disorderly and seemingly undirected manner, first one, and then another. They lacked that elevated unity which inspired us to a man, and it was a picture of total bewilderment. Our first lieutenant, on seeing this sight, shouted, "They're beaten already." Now I went down to the gun deck, where there was a thick fog of sweat and humidity. Many men had tossed their jackets on hooks and were standing in their *Maljen* (tricot undershirts).

The scene played out in a surreal manner up to the first shot; a sort of conventional, genuine ease reigned. When I entered the gun deck the men, who had been leaning out the port gunports, automatically turned around. I felt their eyes in the same way as an actor must feel the eyes of the audience at his first performance – their gaze was like a lead weight.

Midshipman Rosenzweig,[12] a very phlegmatic man, was calmly walking about in his rubber boots, about which the men were whispering. I went to my section midshipman, Zehetmayer.[13] He saluted, pointed to Rosenzweig and said with a laugh, "Those'll do him a lot of good if we have to swim for it!" and I laughed too. But only with my mouth. I thought of the devastation I had seen on the *Schwarzenberg* in 1864, thinking it inevitable we would be brought to that exact state in a short time. It is a peculiar feeling to talk to another man and think: perhaps you will be dead in an hour; perhaps I will be, or perhaps both of us will be. But we laughed nonetheless, and all the men grinned too, but it was a very troubled grin, nothing more than heavy breathing. For then not a shot had sounded, and the intoxication of battle had not then been aroused. Midshipman Zehetmayer pointed to his low shoes and said, "I'm ready if we have to go swimming." We were suddenly convinced that the Italian ironclads would ram us wooden vessels.

Just then up came Midshipman Lorenz[14] and solemnly showed us three fingers. He was a good if somewhat simple chap who had one belief, that he was destined to take part in six actions. He had fought at Heligoland and had taken part in the Sylt expedition, and so he showed me his fingers and said, "My third." At once he became cheerful, shaking everybody's hand and saying, "I congratulate you on your baptism of fire." "The devil," shouted Zehetmayer, "if we have to be, you'll be baptized first," and again we laughed. But then the gun deck commander drew his sabre and raised it, as if to say, "I know why you're making such a noise, but enough's enough," and nodded. Everyone hastened to their posts.

Although the sea had been polished by the rainbow, nonetheless scraps of foam emerged.

Deep silence now reigned. So as to occupy themselves, the gun commanders took pull ropes in their hands and put them down again, then pushed things here and there. Many men were leaning out far, as before, whispering as before. The infantrymen were moving about, examing the handspikes under the carriages. We heard the men moving about on deck above us. All of a sudden there blared the command "Attention": the heads jerked back in and those lying down got up. The engines shook perceptibly as we held our

---

was hesitant about involving his ships in a fight with the Austrian ironclads, that the action was too rapid for him to intervene, and that he nursed a grudge against the commander of the fleet. Be that as it may, the Italian wooden vessels were indeed by and large spectators of the action.

12 Midshipman Julius Rosenzweig.
13 Midshipman Viktor Zehetmayer.
14 Midshipman Franz Lorenz.

breath: they were at full power. We meant to stay as close behind the fast ironclads as we could, at full speed, in order to speed through the Italian enfilading fire.

The pause which followed seemed endless.

All at once the dull report of a heavy gun rolled from outside, and in the rumble of its echo a second, and then a third, the loud, far-off booming increasing. The Italians fired with great haste at the wedge as it rushed along, always firing individually, while we as before steamed forward silently, voraciously. The gun commanders adjusted their sights automatically, even though there was no enemy to be seen and a range had not been ordered. Drops of rain drizzled down from the wet deck, shimmering down the gunports. But soon there was heard a dull rumbling, as if giant fists were beating a colossal bronze door in wild confusion, ever more heavily, and then we understood: it was the first broadside of an Austrian ship. In the middle of this deafening noise, this abnormal thunder, a broadside crashed out, a heavy roar and a briefer reverberation – *Ferdinand Max* had broken through the Italian line. Now there followed at regular intervals the other imperial ironclads. The enemy gunshots thundered over and over, like a raging sea, and over and over they were replied to by short broadsides.

12

The Battle of Lissa, 20 July 1866

The navigator shouted down the speaking tube to the gun deck, "Port side, individual fire beginning with the first gun!", and then "Five cables – four cables!"[1] Several Italian ironclads, driven to one side by Tegetthoff's breakthrough, were advancing at us, but still we saw nothing – as the sun had beamed down earlier, so now did the glistening raindrops. The order was repeated one after another by the commanders, first that of the gun deck in a deep, calm voice, and then the divisional, then the section commanders. The naval infantrymen leaned on the handspikes. In the following silence, nothing was seen clearly but the ends of the guns, lying like waiting bronze beasts to bar the way to the approaching enemy. The 12 gun commanders bent over their guns, their fists on the ball at the end of the barrel so as to fire one after the other.

Then the first Italian passed by at speed; like all the others, she had been painted light grey. In an instant our most forward gun went off, and a flash of lightning lit the gun deck. The crews rushed to the recoiling cannon and ran them back; it was the work of a second for a man to thrust his wet swab into the barrel. Then shot after shot crashed out – smoke puffed, veiling the figures. The fire of the first division of the gun deck ran from fore to aft, flashing out and angling forward, like faces pressing out of the shadows. I leaped to the side of my nearest gun commander, cautioning, "Don't fire if you can't see anything," but a puff of smoke was already driving the dense fumes away, and now my division too blasted away its shells. The enemy ironclad did not reply; she seemed to have either expended her fire on the imperial ships ahead of us or was reloading. The few shots she did fire whistled through *Adria*'s rigging, and you could plainly hear pieces of wood falling onto the deck over us. I saw one of the enemy's guns rising crazily like a dark spot higher, ever higher; I thought to myself, they're shooting terribly, that'll be over our masts. However, it was nearly a hit, for then the gun dropped like a falling bough and a shot fell into the sea beside the frigate with a heavy crash, causing a massive spout of water which drove a torrential, storm-whipped spray through the gun deck. At the same time an Austrian shell exploded against the Italian's hull with a clear flash; her anchor fell, dangling from its chain, and the smoke of the explosion covered practically the entire vessel. As quickly as she had arrived, this enemy vessel was gone. Lieutenant Goritscheck[2] of the naval infantry ran down from above. "Things are going well," he reported, "the Italian line's been broken and the enemy is steaming around without direction, as if they're mad. Some more of them are approaching us." A sailor who had just loaded a round pointed in front of him with his rammer and shouted lustily, "Our boys are coming, our boys are coming."

We looked out the ports and saw four vessels, at their head a remarkably large Italian ironclad, and right behind her a second. They were steaming slowly, as if they were lying in wait and menacing us, saying, "We mean to let you wooden ships feel our more

---

1   914.5–732 m; 1,000–800 yds.
2   Junior Lieutenant Franz Goritschek.

SCHLACHT bei LISSA

Admirals –
Panzer – } Schiffe der Österreicher
Holz =

Admirals –
Panzer – } Schiffe der Italiener
Holz –
beim Beginn der Schlacht.

Namen der größeren Schiffe

Österreich's:

1 u. 2 Division:
1. Erzh. Ferdinand Max.
2. Habsburg
3. Kaiser Max.
4. Don Juan d'Austria
5. Prinz Eugen
6. Salamander
7. Drache
8. Kaiser
9. Novara
10. Schwarzenberg
11. Adria
12. Donau
13. Radetzky
14. Friedrich
(7 Panzer- u. 7 größere Holzschiffe)
3. Div: 10 Schrauben-Kanonenboote
und Schuner;
Außerdem 3 Raddampfer.
Zusammen 27 Schiffe.

Italien's:

1. Principe di Carignano
2. Castelfidardo
3. Ancona
4. Re d'Italia
5. Palestro
6. S. Martino
7. Re di Portogallo
8. Maria Pia
9. Affondatore
10. Varese
11. Terribile
12. Formidabile
(Nur Panzerschiffe) Außerdem:
14 Holzschiffe, 5 Aviso = u.
3 Transportschiffe.
Zus. 34 Schiffe.

IN LISSA

Kroatien
Dalmatien
Lissa
Spalato
Fiume
Istrien
Triest
Venedig
Ancona
Meer
Adriatisches

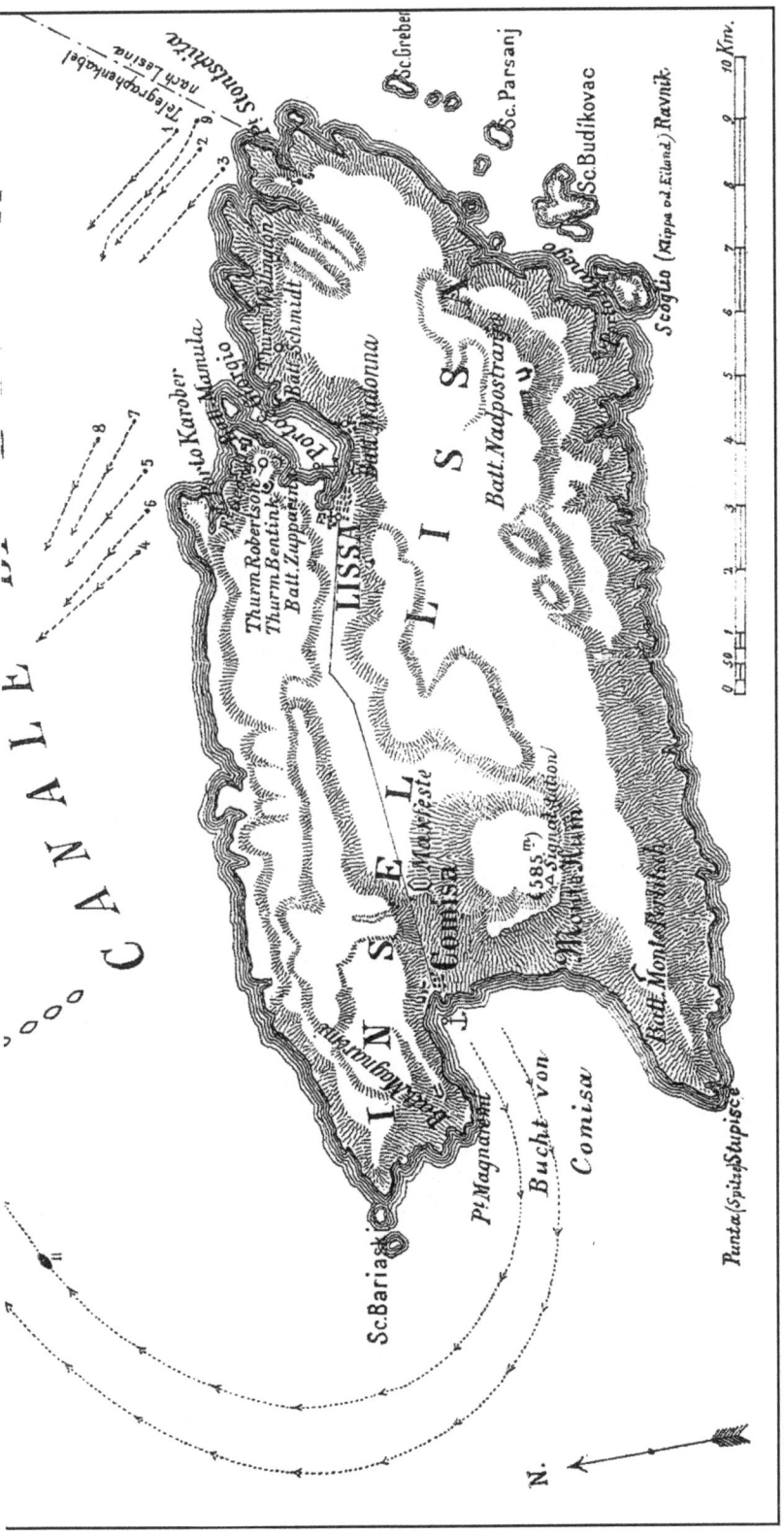

powerful guns." That they had reduced speed considerably so as to be sure of their mark was shown by their small bow waves and limp flags. But the two ironclads pounding after the first two with difficulty were different; they were imperial ones. They seemed curiously small beside the Italians, were painted deep black, and their bow waves covered half their bows, the speed of their movement driving back the many red-white-red flags like streaming hair. The whole picture looked like a furious cow boy was running after two clumsy, trotting oxen, waving his stick.

Once more a command came dully through the speaking tube, and once more it was repeated. Just then the Italians, who had long since passed us by, fired again; something howled over the deck and pieces of rigging clattered down. But now we had the attention of two new enemies, the larger of which I thought was *Re d'Italia* because of her shape and broadside. Flash on flash, shot on shot were exchanged as we passed by on parallel courses. Between the crashing shots was the hubbub of the shouts of command, the rumbling of the guns as they rolled back, the hurrying of the ammunition numbers, and then all at once there sounded a heavy bang, as if someone had thrown open a door. The deck trembled beneath our feet and seemed to rise, and the infantry lieutenant was thrown against me. Almost at the same time the air burst asunder with a shattering explosion – we had taken a direct hit. Pieces of the shattered chain armour rained through the scuppers, whizzing around; smoke the colour of manure climbed rapidly from the waterline, mingling with the smoke of the guns. I saw one man, who the moment before had been stock still, slammed against the side like a puppet on strings. Another reeled about as if drunk, and several others grabbed him. They dragged him away, his arms hanging limply and his undershirt soaked with blood. I asked Goritschek to go and look at the half deck, because that was where the shell had exploded.

While he ran down to do so, we kept up our fire. I was paying special attention to a sailor I had previously thought slipshod. Accustomed to the lively to-and-fro movements of the southern sailors, I had underestimated him, one of the few Germans, for now I saw that his sleepy, quiet manner was just the opposite of cowardice. He was ramming down the swab, a most dangerous job which required him to be extremely close to the gunport. When the gun went off, he was literally hurled in the air. But once on his feet, he tidied himself up and once more zealously and silently worked his swab. In so doing he projected more than half his body into the air. I shouted, "Watch out – you'll fall into the water!" "Why?" he asked, unable to comprehend. He went about his business as if he had done nothing all his life but fight battles.

Now the lieutenant crashed up from the half deck and whispered briefly to the gun deck commander, who waved his hand at me – "Follow him!" Goritschek ran to my side. "What's the matter?" In a low voice he said, "We're listing. We need quick and reliable men to go down to the pumps; the shells have been set on fire and the antechamber of the magazine is burning." The aft ammunition lift now had to be stopped, for it could no longer supply us. I grabbed two infantrymen from each gun. At first they did not want to leave their posts, but when I ordered, "To the pumps, to the pumps," that did the trick and they ran off.

A few seconds later, as we stood in the gun deck without anything to do, we could hear how hard the pumps were working and smell something burning from the hatchways. The end of the sailcloth net in which ammunition was drawn up was burning, and the wet woollen blankets which had been thrown over the glowing wooden and metal parts of the antechamber were smouldering.

The *Re d'Italia* fired again, missed and passed by with her escort, which did not fire. Since we were then totally defenceless, we took her inaction as a real gift from heaven, and with satisfaction I saw them pass by. But then the silent one hesitated, steered up and posted herself so that she was eight cables[3] off our stern, the crowned arms of Savoy plainly visible on her figurehead. I counted eight stubby, sinister barrels slowly swinging towards the *Adria*. They looked soulless and spiteful, iron fingers which halted their fumbling movement and pointed at our deck.

The pumps pounded beneath our feet; at any moment we could be blown into the air by the explosion of our magazine, at any moment we could be mowed down by the eight enemy guns. There was a heaviness in my chest; as if hypnotized I gazed at the eight black mouths, and I would be lying if I did not say I was afraid. A disaster seemed inevitable, but only two of the enemy's guns were loaded. They flashed; one of the shells flew over the deck, the other hit the waterline and exploded. Once more the planks of the deck leaped, people swayed and it was if someone had boxed your ears.

Soon thereafter the infantrymen ran over to me, beaming with joy. The fire in the antechamber had been extinguished, and the small fire the second explosion had caused had been put out right away. "Good, good," one of them laughed. Now, as the men were stooping to the handspikes they had left, Lieutenant Goritschek rushed down the stairs. With sash flapping and chinstrap tight, he thrust his sabre towards the stern and yelled at the top of his lungs, "An Italian's sinking!" repeating the shout in Italian so as to make the men understand. In a flash everyone was at the gunports.

Six to seven cables[4] off *Adria*'s stern I saw the tops of three masts with fluttering tricolours diving into the sea and disappearing. Beside them, seemingly paralyzed, was an Austrian ironclad. Only her flags were moving, as if she was reflecting on the victim of the death struggle. It was the *Re d'Italia* sinking.

For a moment there was dead silence, but then a shot crashed from the ironclad, followed by others, increasing to an uproar, and now the men understood. A cheer rang through the gun deck, and I recall in particular how one naval infantryman swung his handspike in one hand and his cap in the other, stamping his feet and thundering ever more loudly his wild "Urrara, Urrara!", distorting his moustached, Cossack-like face as if he wanted to perform a war dance.

At that moment, the imperial ironclads I mentioned earlier came up with our former opponents. With one to starboard and the other somewhat to port, they crashed out two broadsides one after the other, but then all of them disappeared.

The bugle call of "Attention" pulled the men back to the guns. "Individual fire from the bow down at four cables!" yelled the speaking tube, and the repeating commands buzzed to and fro. A fourth Italian approached, firing at us as she passed by on an opposite course, and soon the enemy vessel exchanged shot for shot with an Austrian frigate which ran in front of us. As the bluish grey smoke disappeared out the gunports, the guns were once more run forward – you heard the rumble of the carriages. Then a sudden jerk, then another, then several together, and then one more. Now the cannon were aimed and made ready to fire. As the enemy ran down the line of frigates, the shots crashed out ever louder.

---

3   1.5 km; .91 mile.
4   1.1–1.3 km; .7–.8 mile.

Now you saw her bow through the port, and now her hull. A line of fire and a chain of gunshots in quick succession swept down the deck. The men had become used to the appearance of the enemy by now, and they fired as if they were on exercise. It we had had better guns the Italians would have suffered severely, but it was if we were throwing dried peas against a wall. The enemy's flank looked to have been dotted with indentations, but what harm did that do her!

But for all that, she could again hit *Adria*, and two or three rounds through the gunports once more placed her in danger. Flames were ablaze in our sail depot below, as I learned half an hour later. The danger was just as great as it had been the first time, for the stores of paint and oil were kept beside the depot, and if the fire had reached them it would have been uncontrollable. But after a fairly long time, this blaze too was mastered. Suffice it to say *Adria* was set on fire by this direct hit; the old wooden frigates cannot fight in modern times as marvellously as they then did, and it was their last battle in the history of the world.

After the Italian went by, the first phase of the battle ended for us. In three wedges, the Austrian fleet had stormed through the enemy ironclads, forcing them to port and starboard. The latter, chased by the Austrian ironclads, which had turned back, had then thrown themselves against the wooden ships and were passing close by in a gun duel. Everything which I have described at length occurred as the enemy went by, but it was played out very quickly. Now the action died away to such an extent that to our rear the combat of the ironclads was wasting powder and was at a stand. However, the wooden frigates steamed on towards Lissa.

They did so because of a fairly remarkable action between three Italians, *Affondatore*, *Re di Portogallo* and *Maria Pia*,[5] and the *Kaiser*, flagship of the wooden division, and they attacked her one after the other, pounding her into a sorry state. We now hastened to her aid, she at that time being repeatedly threatened by *Affondatore*.

The drums rattled "Man starboard guns," and with a confusion of thuds and a rushing of feet the men flew to the other side. Now a barbaric sight unfolded before us, a battle of giants to the death. To one side lay *Affondatore*, quite low in the water and very long, apparently once more trying for a mortal ramming strike. But she always shrank from it, falling back and firing with her powerful turret guns. The fear of not being able to free herself from *Kaiser* in time to prevent her being dragged down with her enemy checked her.

Yet *Kaiser* looked horrible. Three times taller than her iron tormentor, she wobbled to starboard, and then to port, dragging herself slowly towards the harbour's shelter. A mast had fallen, the funnel had been destroyed and many small fires wrapped her hull in smoke from the deck to the waterline. In short, the battleship was nothing more than a gigantic burning cloud, over which improbably floated the huge red-white-red flag of the remaining mast. This mass of vapour, in which men wrestled with death and flames, wallowed towards the rocky island.

But although we presumed that sooner or later *Kaiser* would blow up, although she was being towed by an imperial gunboat which was fishing out the drowning one, she kept firing. The battleship crashed out unbroken broadsides towards the *Affondatore*, sending dazzling bands of lightning through the hellish smoke in her hull.

---

5   *Regina Maria Pia*, to give the full name, was one of a class of four broadside ironclads. Launched in 1863, she displaced 4 250 tonnes, had 26 guns and 480 crew. Rebuilt between 1888 and 1890, she was stricken in 1904.

Thus we wooden vessels hastened to her aid, forming a line ahead as we joined one another. Moving slowly, a band of flags with high sides seemingly wrinkled by the chains overlaid on them, we steamed towards the Italian. *Kaiser* had by then more or less left my sight, and now followed the minutes in which I heard the heaviest thunder of cannon, for all the frigates fired concentrically on *Affondatore*, a continuous shower of white gun smoke. She barely had fallen away towards the sea when new clouds of smoke swept over her, to sink and be replaced by the next ones. In a short time, *Adria* alone blazed about a hundred rounds at the enemy ironclad. On the frigates, the correct course was to depress the guns as low as possible and load with solid shot, and thus we tried to attack the Italian's unarmoured deck.

As in old pictures a siege is artlessly depicted, so goes this part of the battle, the blue sky being saturated with shot for moments at a time. *Affondatore* vanished into the scattering foam of the projectiles which hailed down into the sea around her. Sometimes she replied to the attack with interest, and then like pointed tongues of fire her guns would flash their beams out of the cloaking veil of water. But then she suddenly went silent, and shortly thereafter shot out of the storm, waves boiling at her bow, to fall on *Kaiser*. She obviously now wanted to give the death stroke and had forgotten all her past hesitation. But halfway there she slowed, turned about and steamed off. The official Italian report states that the captain and first lieutenant were seriously determined to destroy the imperial battleship before they broke off the action, which was just then coming to an end and which move would have been to no purpose, but that Admiral Count Persano[6] had forced them to desist from this daring deed under the threat of a court martial.

"Halt" was blown on the imperial wooden ships. While now only the rifled guns of the upper deck fired on *Affondatore* at extreme elevation, we officers climbed up into the sun from the silent gun deck. You looked about you. The *Kaiser*, a fiery cloud, was at the head of our line, and dense smoke was blowing out of the gunports of the other vessels. To our rear the ironclads were in action, and *Affondatore* was hastening there. I was just talking with the navigator when out crashed one of our smoothbore guns; the gun commander could not bear to have his gun be silent. "What kind of idiotic behaviour is this?" the navigator shouted. And now the captain[7] too saw how the shot of the overzealous man had raised a small column of water halfway to *Affondatore*. He was beside himself with rage – "I'll have him shot!" he yelled. Officers and men of the upper gun deck threw themselves on the unfortunate, who had a stupid face, and treated him to blows on his ribs.

Now you looked once more at *Kaiser*, our commander. She could no longer signal and was silent, reeling and burning, so we no longer had a commander. But Tegetthoff's spirit had such a strong influence on the wills of the officers and on their speedy appraisal of the situation, that all at once all the frigates turned, as if in some mysterious manner they had received orders to leave the badly wounded vessel. As fast as we could, we steamed towards the ironclads, while *Kaiser* dragged herself towards the island. Although I have mentioned the inadequacy of the wooden frigates in modern times shortly before, although we could be hit over and over again and set on fire, although we had an opponent of like

---

6   Carlo Count Pellion di Persano (1806–83), the Italian admiral in command during the battle. He is generally thought to have conducted the battle in an uncertain, indeed incompetent, manner. His transfer to *Affondatore* occurred just before the action opened, and many Italian captains thought he was still on *Re d'Italia*.

7   Captain Adolf Daufalik commanded the *Adria* during the battle.

force (the Italian wooden ships, which lay idly there off the island), in a trice we threw ourselves into the unequal contest, for there the battle was to be decided.

In order to carry out this decision, there sufficed but a short conversation on *Adria* between the captain and navigator, something which may have occurred on the other frigates as well. Without mutual agreement, the ships turned as if at a blow and steamed towards the chaos of the ironclads – I say chaos because it was one in the fullest sense of the word. The sky and the sea were completely blue; only on the far western horizon were rainbows. In the clear, sunny day a thick, sharply defined cloud of smoke was suspended over the water: coal smoke and smoke from the guns of the combatants, who drove pell-mell against one another as if they were mad, crowded together at the closest ranges. You could not make out any details; only flags were to be seen.

And the interior of this compact, roaring clump of dense smoke was continuously lit on the inside by a flashing, such as a cloudbank charged with electricity in heavy weather. From time to time there would shoot out a grey or black ship, as if it had been forced out into the bright day by a hit, but then it would hold for a second and then in an instant disappear back into the turmoil.

Passing the Italian wooden vessels, which sped by without firing, we rushed towards the confusion. I descended into the gun deck and looked forward with some brother officers. We commented that *Affondatore* had escaped with no damage at all, since our arching fire seemed to have been to no purpose, but in fact, while at Ancona she succumbed to her injuries and sank.[8] While we were entertaining ourselves, parts of chains which had been ripped free rattled as *Adria* moved, and from time to time the upper deck guns boomed.

Then the bugles blared and the drums rolled once more. The ammunition numbers stood ready beside the hoists with new cartridges, and the gun commanders were bending over their barrels. But it was impossible to fire, for the ironclad melee began to move towards the rear, towards the northwest. Black ships rushed by fighting; grey ones were visible only briefly. Just before the imperial wooden ships could become embroiled in the chaos, just before we in the lower deck could join in the fire of the upper deck guns, which were firing ever more quicker, the distance increased. Then there was a gigantic movement; the speed became faster, and all at once the grey vessels broke out to assemble, in their midst one whose stern was a huge blaze.

In a second you saw two large clouds of smoke, one of black and one of grey ships, like two clouds rolling one behind the other. Simultaneously *Ferdinand Max* rushed by signalling "Assemble." While the Italian ironclads ran for the open sea, while their wooden ships sailed for them, Tegetthoff had had formed three parallel lines, the first of the ironclads, and then the wooden frigates, and finally the gunboats. While we very slowly assembled, the enemy turned anew in confused groups at a distance of two to three nautical miles[9] and once more opened a rapid fire. We replied slowly and calmly. Between the two groups there steamed the burning Italian, helpless and smoking.

Once more the batteries of the wooden frigates were ordered to cease fire, and for them everything which followed was like a play. The rifled guns above fired, supporting the ironclads, who were so to speak leisurely avoiding the last despairing movement of the enemy to continue the battle. The latter fired worse than at the start, and frequently

---

8   While Rottauscher's claim is plausible, another and perhaps more convincing reason for the *Affondatore's* sinking is that she had a very low freeboard and was swamped by the waves.

9   4–5.6 km; 2.7–3.4 miles.

and curiously, shells fired into the air exploded with flashes and small clouds. Many people swore they were shrapnel shells, which of course we could not confirm, but yet they might have been.

In a word, the men of the gun deck sat down, dragged over the small tubs and began to eat and drink. They were all pleased, for even the sailors could see that it had very clearly been an Austrian victory: here were our ships, close together and keen, ordered exactly as if on a chessboard, there the confusion of the Italians and their burning ironclad. A joyful buzz went around.

On the ships of this period a room of the captain's cabin was set aside to be equipped with guns, and in order that the men at these guns could hear orders more quickly, before the battle the bulkhead was broken down with axes. A background of devastation for the gun deck – three easy chairs lay about, and a credenza had been smashed by a projectile. Now we officers rushed there and plundered happily in the wreckage – some bottles of wine and packages of ship's biscuit had escaped the shell. We got them out, sat ourselves at an unoccupied gunport and chatted. First we criticized the inaccurate fire of the Italians, for if a shot fell close by, the next one was further on. Then we talked about how our ironclads had rammed, and we made bets that *Ferdinand Max* was missing its figurehead. The others looked in a ruinous state, but these damages were less dangerous than they seemed, destroyed boats hanging from their hulls, devastated rigging and funnels shot through to such a degree that wisps of smoke were rising from them.

We debated whether the Italians would attack again, because Tegetthoff at least did not seem to have any malicious joy for such an action, and then suddenly a signal climbed the mast of *Ferdinand Max*. We read: "Report damages, dead and wounded." In an instant we recognized that the chance of a renewed action hung on the favourable or unfavourable answers about them. Everyone on *Adria* hoped for the best and were pleased we could report light losses, but despite that we felt a certain shame. Only seven men had been killed – might we not be accused of keeping out of the action? But what was our astonishment as a result when only a few other ships reported a greater figure and many a lower figure, and indeed one frigate was pleased to let the flag for nought flutter in the wind. In the meantime, an Austrian ironclad left the line and steamed towards the burning vessel so as to take her off, but she returned with the message that she was lost as it was.

We shouted to each other that Tegetthoff would certainly now advance anew and bravely asserted that the battle had gone so splendidly. The Italians, who simultaneously recognized their ironclad's difficult situation, launched boats. Several of them made their way towards the burning vessel, which as we learned in Fasana from newspapers was the *Palestro*.[10] Signals were flying up and down her mast all the time. A large boat had just reached the ill-fated ship when a brown cloud burst from her stern. We clapped our glasses to our eyes. The mizzen mast folded in on itself and crashed forward, burying the funnel; the cloud spread rapidly and swept towards the bow. Now we saw a huge stab of flame spring up, and then just fire and smoke, with dark spots suspended above like dancing feathers, pieces of wreckage being hurled into the air. When the smoke cleared, there was only disturbed water at the spot. The boats, which had gotten close in the meantime, sailed about searching; others shot towards the scene of the accident with speedy strokes of their oars. The heavy gunfire had not allowed the sound of the explosion to reach our

---

10 Launched in 1862, the *Palestro* was one of two iron gunboats included in the battle line at Lissa. She was 2 200 tonnes, had 4 guns and a crew of 250.

ears, but now there was a breathless pause as everyone went quiet, and then followed cheers of jubilation. For the longest time, after one cheer had died away another broke out of the gunports of a distant and drifted across to us. The long-range artillery action which then began again mingled its thundering with their celebrating. "Now a second one," Midshipman Lorenz laughed, "that's finished them off."

But we did not attack, instead slipping along extremely slowly and still in the same formation, while some of the Italian ships fired and others searched for survivors. Perhaps Tegetthoff wanted to give them the chance to save the men if they could. To be brief, the spectacle of the cruising boats and the fairly ineffective exchange of fire lasted half an hour, and so the duel flagged. Finally the gunfire had become so infrequent that often there were long pauses between shots. Once the Italians finally recovered their boats, they fell back still further, and then gradually steamed away. One of their vessels turned towards the open sea, followed at intervals by the others in a desultory muddle. Then all was still.

Tegetthoff ordered the gunboats to run into Lissa, and the small ships steamed for the harbour in a long line, we others keeping watch. It was thought the enemy was still considering what to do, and as a result everyone was filled with amazement when the battle was really seen to be over. Crowded together, the Italian squadron made off towards the horizon without a pause, and soon it was only a low, thick bank of cloud over the sea. *Ferdinand Max* signalled "Second Division to Lissa!", and we wooden frigates followed the gunboats. The bugles sounded the retreat and the powder magazines were closed, and at once everyone lit a cigarette and began to smoke cheerfully. Then up rolled to me a Venetian sailor, dancing with joy. "Tobacco, sir," he begged, "tobacco." The other sailors too pressed about us with the same request, for most of their supply had been burned with the half deck. We gave what we had to spare, and there was a secret, respectable joy. The men did not ask about the victory or the enemy – their main concern was they had survived the battle safe and sound, and most of all that they could now smoke again. This is no criticism of them; they were brave men who had done their duty.

We officers climbed on deck and discussed the battle. Pieces of rigging were so devastated it was as if a hurricane had hit them. On many ships, even the flags at the tops of the masts were shot through, but there were few hits to their hulls. Once more we looked back at our ironclads; they were still in line ahead and watching the Italians, who were now little more than a thin cloud. Tegetthoff did not pursue them, for their engines were more powerful. He could not assume airs, and they had a head start on him.

It was mid-afternoon when the wooden frigates slid slowly through the harbour entrance. The landscape was bizarre, as in a book of fairy tales; there was a shoal before the entrance, the cliffs were high and stony, and the coast was edged with the white spray of the deep blue sea. The fires on *Kaiser* had been put out, but still wandering captive wisps of smoke appeared here and there among the rocky slopes, flitting from the glowing wood and tar.

Artillerymen moved through the wreckage of the devastated coastal batteries. Many sat silently beside overturned guns, as if they could not comprehend they had escaped the end which had menaced them; others stood bolt upright, their legs wide apart, waving their caps and cheering us. A tower had burst down to its foundations. The closer we looked, the more the traces of the bombardment of the preceding days came to light. Beside the wreck of the *Kaiser* the tops of the masts of the Lloyd steamer *Egytto*[11] protruded from the still harbour – her captain had sunk her when the enemy had steamed in.

The wooden frigates moored close together before the houses of Kut, and the ironclads followed an hour later, anchoring in the entrance. During the evening, the dead and badly wounded were disembarked in silent boats. Such was my view of the battle of Lissa, which will be one of the most remarkable in naval warfare because of its setting, the nature of the enemy and our commander, as well for its contrast of old and new.

---

11   The steamer *Egitto* had been built between 1861 and 1863 and had been chartered by the navy in 1866 as a transport, at 1 490 tonnes and 126 crew. On 19 July she was sunk as a blockship in the entrance to Lissa harbour. Raised and taken over by the navy as the *Gargnano* transport and hospital ship, she was hulked in 1890 and broken up two years later.

13

In the harbour of Lissa

A black cloud awaited the victims of the battle on shore and searched for information about relatives, for if an inhabitant of Lissa was in the military he would be in the navy. There was one woeful scene during this apprehensive reception. An old fisherman had hastened to the shore to ask about his son, who was a helmsman on the *Kaiser*, and the first boat to land from that ship brought his mutilated corpse. The sobbing greybeard had to be dragged away by main force or else he might not have been separated from the bloody linen which covered the remains.

The workmen hammered all night making the wooden coffins, an unpleasant music in the wordless silence. The next morning, a fine violet mist floated lightly and aimlessly over the sea, which was steeped in blue. We went ashore and walked along the beach to the other side of the harbour, where lay the settlement of Lissa. As we did we passed the Madonna battery.[1] Once the other fortifications had been destroyed it had been attacked by four Italian ironclads, one of which had fired on the battery at 300 metres[2] range. After a brief battle, the Italian vessel took a direct hit, lost 40 men and had to abandon its anchor chain so as to quickly reach the harbour entrance, and it was followed by the other three. The battery, which lay right above the road, had not suffered much. However, the road was, so to speak, ploughed up, and the olive grove above the guns looked as if it had been devastated by a storm, its trees in splinters, smashed here and there, and everything saturated to far away with broken branches.

Our next port of call was the hospital, where lay about 50 badly wounded artillerymen and about 60 sailors, not just in the rooms but in the entrance hall and crowded together on the landing. They were covered with blankets, and most were listless. The rooms smelled of carbolic acid. Every man had a palm or olive branch, which he flapped half-heartedly from time to time to keep away the flies. For the latter, drawn by the flowing blood, had gathered in disgusting masses, making an evil noise with their buzzing and swarming in the silence of the hospital.

To our astonishment, an orderly told us that not far from the hospital there were housed 20 prisoners, some of the survivors from *Re d'Italia*. They had clung to a spar and had been in the water from morning to midnight, eventually swimming to the island at Comisa.[3] Peasants had taken up the exhausted men and triumphantly bore them to Lissa, over the mountains, over stony roads in total darkness. We also visited these poor men. They lay on their beds in the deathlike sleep of total exhaustion, mouths open and faces greenish pale. We put cigarettes and eatables on the edges of their beds. As we were

---

1   The Madonna Battery, constructed during the 1830s, took a prominent part in resisting the Italian assault. On the 19th, when four Italian ironclads entered the harbour and engaged the Austrian works, the battery successfully fought off one enemy ship and forced her and her consorts to leave.
2   313 yds.
3   Komiža.

leaving, one of them awoke, fumbled at his presents and murmured in a Neapolitan accent, "Ah, gentlemen, it was better under Francesco the Second."[4]

When we returned to the ship at 1400 hours, *Ferdinand Max* raised a vice admiral's flag – Tegetthoff had been promoted. All the ships fired a salute, and from the shrouds all the men cheered the victor. At the same time, His Majesty's thanks were made known to us by a signal.

I must now recount what I learned about the catastrophe to *Re d'Italia*, whose loss had been nothing more to me than a fleeting impression of masts sinking in powder smoke. An officer on Tegetthoff's staff said that they had twice tried to ram, but in vain, and that the third time a flag had been torn from an Italian. Just then the admiral's personal adjutant was hit and fell against a rail, while Sterneck, the captain of *Ferdinand Max*, was hanging from a shroud in the smoke and looking ahead. Suddenly he ordered full speed, and shortly thereafter "All stop." Tegetthoff shouted "Bravo!" and there was heard from the bow a crash as the ship rammed into the flank of *Re d'Italia*. You saw in unbelievable detail its masts and funnel, heard Italian shouts of command and the roll of drums calling on the enemy to board. On *Ferdinand Max* it was as if the ship were climbing a mountain, but notwithstanding not a man fell to his knees at the impact. The Italian first rolled completely to one side, and then bounded back, pieces of her masts catapulting off as she did so. She seemed to be guzzling the nearby waves into her darkening breach at one gulp. The *Re d'Italia* sank very fast.

Many, however, were stunned as the opposing deck angled towards them in that first moment; men streamed against one another, many running towards the rail, some in strange postures and starting to slip as they fired their rifles at *Ferdinand Max*. Many men rushed towards the stern in order to strike the flag, but a midshipman was clutching its sheet, and he shot down the people with a revolver in order than the ship should sink honourably. This brave man was named Razzetti. In the total confusion, the guns tore loose, rolled down, upturned and leaped over the deck, crushing everything in their way and tearing whole lanes. Just as the Italian sank, the foamy sea was spotted with blue dot after blue dot, for the men not drowned in the ship's bowels had begun to swim. These dots swiftly disappeared as the men undressed smartly. Tegetthoff was going to lower boats when an enemy ironclad came in for a ramming stroke of its own. "It seems to me," the admiral said, "that it's our turn now." But by a skilful manoeuvre, *Ferdinand Max* fell away, and the two vessels passed down each other's sides. The gun-deck officers screamed to the men to fire, and many of them waited impatiently at the gun ports to fire pistols. However, the guns had fired a broadside shortly before, and although the loaders worked away they were not in time, and so they banged the enemy's armour with the ends of their rammers.

An officer of *Habsburg*, which right after the catastrophe steamed by the scene of the sinking, told me appalling things. The naked men had seized pieces of wood, and it was awful to hear through the thunder of the guns the howling of the drowning men, who were screaming for mercy. Bending down, this officer saw one man trying despairingly to get away before he was chopped in pieces by *Habsburg*'s propellor. The distorted face of the unhappy man turned to him was, however, swept into the sucking whirl. A sailor on the gun deck was seized with a rush of blood to the head at the sight of the hundreds

---

4 (1836–94), the last ruler of the Neapolitan kingdom, deposed in 1861.

of helpless men and, dancing about, shouted for cartridges. Only a blow from an officer brought him to reason.

As far as the second catastrophe, that of *Palestro*, is concerned, there was an argument about which ship had had the honour to set her on fire with a shot. The correct reason for her loss may well be what an Italian officer told me in Canea.[5] Coal had been heaped in the stern and a large number of shells placed in the gun decks. An Austrian shell set some coal alight, and broadsides continuously swept away members of the fire-fighting parties. Eventually the fire grew, encompassed the shells, and finally the magazine. It should be noted that this description of events went around the Italian officer corps because of the report of a midshipman who was the sole survivor of *Palestro*'s officers.

Austrian losses were about 180 dead and wounded,[6] half of them on *Kaiser*, for the enemy took her triangular commodore's flag to mean she was Tegetthoff's ship. Within 15 minutes she was burning on all sides, the dead lying about and whole sections of her sides smashed in. *Kaiser* forced her way through by ramming *Re di Portogallo*, thereby losing her foremast, which fell onto the deck, and she slid off the enemy's armour, scraping down the gun decks which had fired a moment before. If the Italian gunners had not loaded with blanks in the confusion then reigning, there would have been a butchery, but nothing happened but powder smoke and burns.

I set foot on this vessel and found the destruction which I had seen on *Schwarzenberg* increased to the highest degree. The wood was charred or begrimed by flames, and the traces of blood, which many times showed red on the planks around an entire gun position, made an impression not easily forgotten. An enemy shot had traversed the length of the second deck from stern to bow, and its route could be seen by the furrow about 15 cm[7] deep through the planking, and you saw plainly by the splashes of blood on the deck above as well as by the lighter traces of blood on the sides how it had cut down those in its path. There two badly wounded midshipman lay together on cots, for there was no more room in the hospital. I squatted between them and heard what they related with shining eyes, although often interrupted by their weakness. How they had been wreathed in fire and fumes, how the concentric broadsides had crashed out against the enemy in smoke and fire, how every second they expected the ship would be torn apart by an explosion. How a drummer leaned against the side, his blood flowing from his forehead to such a degree that he could no longer see, but that nonetheless he continued to beat his instrument and did not want to leave his post. The midshipmen also pointed to a corner where a giant shot lay unexploded. When it had entered, several sailors had dashed at it in order to roll it to an officer, calling out continually in amazement, "What a monster!" For it was three times larger than our shot and they had seen it for the first time in their lives.

The funeral of those who had fallen took place in the afternoon. I was on watch and took in the spectacle from my bridge. Two thousand men had been disembarked, and they stood in a long white lane, wearing their lacquered hats, from Kut to the cemetery at Lissa. The sun was already sinking behind the mountains and veiled the road in its many soft shadows. To the sound of music, the coffins were brought from the little garden beside the chapel where they had been stacked, many black, roughly made coffins, many of them very small because they contained only body parts. At their head were carried

---

5   Kandia, Crete.

6   Official loss tallies count 38 killed and 138 wounded.

7   6 in.

the coffins of the dead officers, those of two ship's captains and Midshipman Proch. All were covered with flags.

Of these officers, Moll,[8] commanding *Drache*,[9] had the most singular death. He had locked himself with a midshipman and Weyprecht, the later Arctic explorer, in an armoured turret which was open at the top and only gave protection up to head height. The Italians had just started to fire at the wedge as it stormed along when the near-sighted man took off his glasses, cleaned them and said with a laugh, "So now we'll have a little bit of ramming. But first of all I have to see what we're going to ram." At that moment a shot skimmed over the turret and took off the top of Moll's skull. Weyprecht, spattered with his captain's brains and drenched with his blood, was thrown to one side, but he jumped up and without a moment's hesitation ordered a broadside, this learned man who in his spare time built herbariums with his delicate fingers and examined the workings of insects' antennae.

I looked at the funeral procession until it disappeared beneath the cypresses on the peninsula. The ships fired a muffled salute, their smoke passing over the water of the harbour. Tegetthoff was the first to throw a handful of earth on the coffins; the clods fell, and there was planted the rosemary tree beneath which they now all sleep.

The ships relieved one another on the watch outside, and they brought trophies: parts of masts and a boat, and later also a box of the deputy Boggio[10] was fished out by the gunboat *Reka*. Boggio had been on *Re d'Italia* to send reports to parliament, and he had drowned. The box contained letters, some of them still legible, reporting on the bombardment of the forts, on the brave defence and the brave attack. They were full of Latinate pathos, and one point is especially worthy of mention, for Boggio told how Italy's young naval heroes stood on the poop deck singing patriotic hymns despite the hail of shot from the batteries.

My former commander on the *Saida*, von G., at last crowned his quixotic adventures, and in the most grotesque manner. Sick to death he had not succeeded in ramming and sending to the bottom not 10, not even one, Italian, he was on his bridge when an enemy vessel passed by. G., always motivated by mediaeval chivalry and gallantry, bowed and saluted the enemy captain with an elegant sweep of his cap, who if somewhat taken aback returned the salute in a friendly manner. At that moment a bullet whistled by G's ear. "A rifle!" G. shrieked in indignation, "a rifle! no Italian is going to rub me out!" Everyone on the bridge looked nervously at such a noble savage, who succumbed to such an emotion. The hammer flashed, but no shot followed, the enemy captain bade farewell with a mocking wave of his hand and left G. crushed. He was the last chevalier I knew, one from the time in which one doffed his feathered tricorne hat and called out, "English gentlemen, fire first!"[11]

---

8   Friedrich Freiherr von Moll (born 1829).

9   A sister ship to the *Salamander*, the *Drache* was modernized in 1867/68, stricken in 1883 and broken up in 1895/96.

10 Per Carlo Boggio (1827–66), an ardent expansionist member of the Italian parliament, had embarked on the fleet as commissioner for the lands of the Austrian empire which were expected to be conquered.

11 This quote is from the battle of Fontenoy in 1745, when a French officer said them to Lord Charles Hay, commander of a Guards regiment of the British army. According to a letter he wrote shortly after the battle, Hay replied, "We never fire first; fire yourselves," and the French did, but suffered severely from the British counter-volley.

14

The conclusion of peace

While the Austrian newspapers gave little space to Lissa, the Italian ones trumpeted the battle as a victory for their fleet to the extreme. Our squadron, after a stubborn action, had been forced to flee into the island's harbour, while theirs had steamed to Ancona to pick up fresh ammunition. Two Italian ironclads had certainly gone down, but *Kaiser* too had been sunk, with 1,000 men, 600 of them Tyrolese marksmen, which was especially greatly emphasized. For the Tyrolese are and remain in Italian eyes a bloodthirsty, savage mountain race who eat raw chamois and combine legendary bravery with bestial cruelty. The Tyrolese marksmen perched like swallows on the battleship's spars and caused so many losses that the Italians had but one thought, to destroy this troublesome opponent, which they did. It had been an imposing sight, the sea covered with pointed Ziller valley hats[1] when *Kaiser* went down. An Italian gunboat added to the victory celebrations when she reported that the Austrian fleet was no longer off Lissa. She had come from Taranto to join Persano's squadron on the Dalmatian coast but had found neither friend nor foe, and consequently she had scoured the passages between the islands. When she ran into the harbour of Lesina, the street urchins crawled around the rocky crags, threw stones and shouted jeeringly, "Clear out, clear out, or Tegetthoff'll be on you!" But despite that, the captain's report that he had found no trace of the Austrians sufficed for new cheers to sweep across the kingdom.

Slowly the truth forced its way through, and only with the investigation of the military court which hung over Persano, so that now hatred was begotten which branded us as murderers. Only the fable of the sunken *Kaiser* and of the 600 Tyrolese remained unshaken, consoling the kingdom somewhat for its defeat.

Suddenly, 20 days after the battle, Tegetthoff was summoned to Nebresina,[2] the railway junction above Trieste, to confer with the headquarters of South Army. He put to sea on the yacht *Greif*,[3] and all night the fleet lay cleared for action and ready to sail, for the next morning the ceasefire with Italy ended.[4] The South Army, which had been transferred to the Danube, had turned about and come back, and the course of diplomatic negotiations seemed to indicate that the war would certainly start again. Since we had received good reports about Prussia's love of peace, Venice would now be reunited with Austria and the double eagle would once more fly over the walls of the Lido and Malghera. But morning brought the despatch that the ceasefire was to be extended for four weeks.

The admiral returned. A plan had been devised that when hostilities recommenced the fleet would embark an army corps, land it in the lagoons of Venice and so threaten

---

1   The male inhabitants of the Ziller valley, in northeastern Tyrol, wore distinctive pointed tricorne hats with feather decorations, called *Krapfenhüten*.
2   Aurisinia, Italy.
3   At 1 260 tonnes, *Greif* had been the *Jupiter* steamer of the Austrian Lloyd before being purchased and renamed by the navy in 1860. She served as the imperial yacht until 1884, being present, for example, at the opening of the Suez Canal in 1869.
4   Tegetthoff left on 9 August; the ceasefire was due to expire early on the 11th.

the enemy's flank. Tegetthoff had opposed this unreasonable demand to embark soldiers on his ships as long as there was a squadron in Ancona superior to his, even though three of its ships had been sunk, and he could not see his way to approve his gun decks being crammed with army soldiers.

Nonetheless, on 12 August we left and steamed to Triest in order to anchor close offshore in the Bay of Muggia. The idea of a Venetian expedition still seemed possible. Large masses of men, among them a colourful mixture of uniforms of units we might have to embark in case of war, filled the moles and shores to see the spectacle of the arriving fleet.

This especial inquisitiveness of the population had its roots in the persistent myth about the sinking of the *Kaiser*. Despite its having been denied, everyone, especially those in the Italophile faction, asserted that the *Kaiser* was not among the fleet. When I speak of a faction, I must mention that until 1848 Triest had been so loyal as to have been termed "The Faithful." When, to our disgrace, the Sardinian fleet had blockaded the city a volunteer levee en masse, called the *Bauccoli*, had been formed from men of the region, the elite of the city serving as its officers. And then in 1859, when the new Italy stretched out its claws, there was barely mention of an Italophile faction. But one did indeed exist in 1866. The city fathers and influential men were always good imperialists, for they knew that if the city was joined to the kingdom they would be ruined economically.[5] On the other hand, there were some in whom the pull of kinship won over their fear for their businesses. For we saw in a large book dealer's a picture of the officers of *Re d'Italia* with the caption "The martyrs of Lissa." But to be honest, my anger was directed more at the authorities who had permitted such a thing to happen.

A buzz ran through the masses on the moles and shore when *Kaiser* was seen to be missing. There were the most excited debates in coffeehouses and restaurants, which ended only when the battleship came in sight a few hours later. The work on her freshly raised mast had caused her to be delayed....[6]

In the meantime, rumours had been started about the admiral's imminent fall. On the last day of September he left the fleet to go to foreign parts.[7] All too late did he remain deaf to the falsely extravagant proposals of the United States to enter its service, all too late was he summoned back in order to bring home the corpse of the emperor of Mexico over the ocean, and to be named to take command of the navy for a short period. He died only five years later.

But on this day, as he sailed through the squadron to take leave of it, the tumult broke out again, and just as before the battle men stormed from the bowels of the ships into their rigging. Hundreds of hands reached out to him, as if they wanted to keep him with them, and there was a wild roaring and shouting in the air. But Tegetthoff was no longer the same man as the one who had laughingly thanked the cheers of acclamations. Now he leaned gloomily on the stern of the *Greif* as she bore him towards land, staring ahead, only now and then, when the cheering became too loud, briefly moving his hand to the peak of his cap without looking around. We officers watched him go.

---

5   The point being that Trieste was the empire's main outlet to the sea and its most important port, and that if the city was joined to Italy it would become a backwater with no commercial ties to its natural hinterland. This indeed occurred after 1918, when Trieste became part of Italy.

6   On 13 August, the day the definitive Austro-Italian ceasefire came into effect, the fleet had a review.

7   In November 1866 Tegetthoff started on his mission of inspection; he was on leave until then.

Related titles published by Helion & Company

The Road to Königgrätz. Helmuth von Moltke and the Austro-Prussian War 1866
Quintin Barry
552pp   Hardback
ISBN 978-1-906033-37-8
A limited edition of 750
numbered & signed copies

History of the Campaign of 1866 in Italy
Alexander Hold
176pp   Paperback
ISBN 978-1-906033-62-0

Forthcoming titles

A Bibliography of the Seven Weeks' War of 1866
Stuart Sutherland   ISBN 978-1-906033-64-4

The Contribution of the Royal Bavarian Army to the War of 1866
Bavarian General Staff   ISBN 978-1-906033-66-8

The Organization of the German State Forces in 1866
Stuart Sutherland   ISBN 978-1-906033-68-2

HELION & COMPANY
26 Willow Road, Solihull, West Midlands B91 1UE, England
Telephone 0121 705 3393   Fax 0121 711 4075
Website: http://www.helion.co.uk

Lightning Source UK Ltd.
Milton Keynes UK
UKOW06n1140070515

251060UK00005B/77/P